IN
GOOD
COMPANY

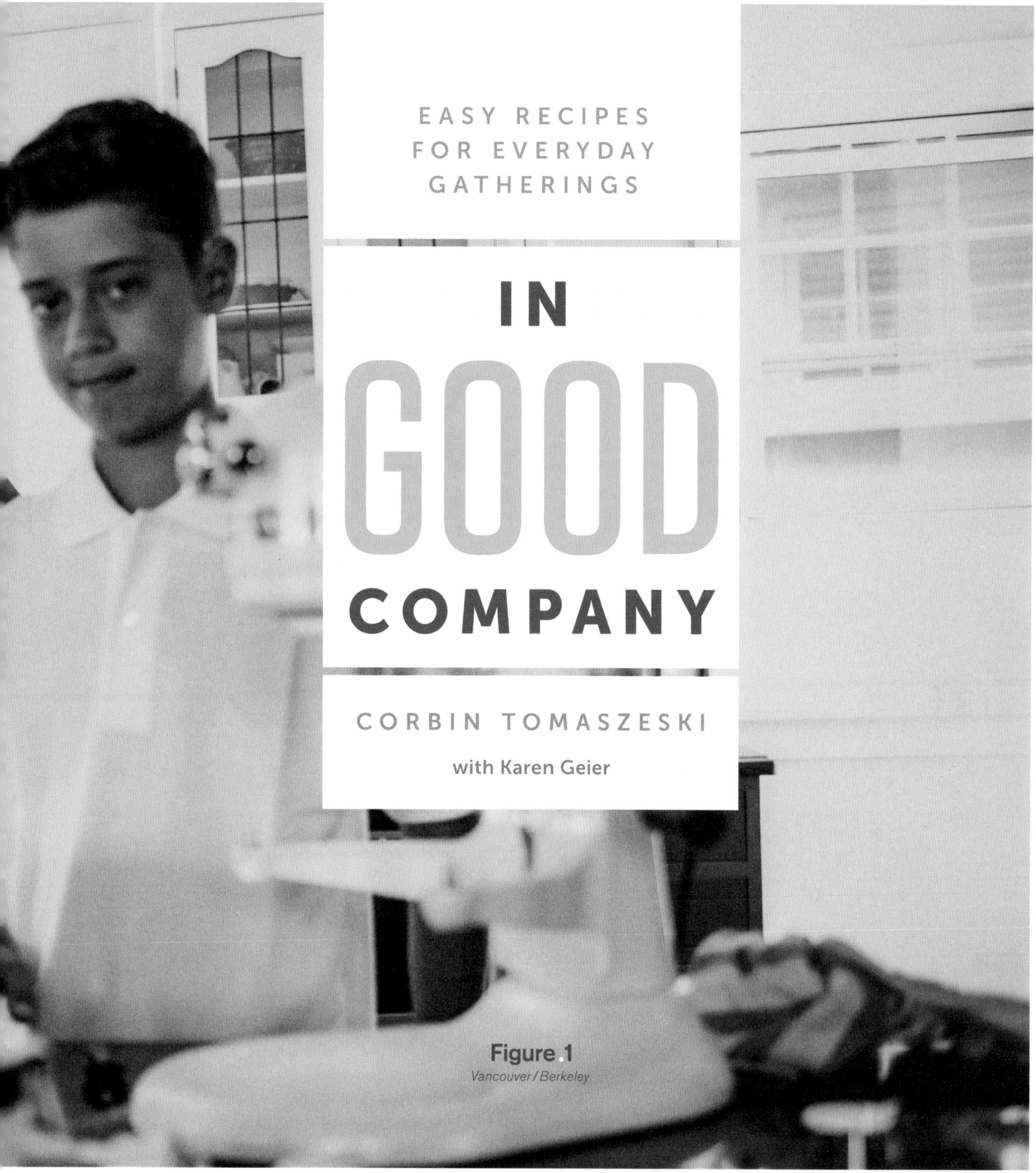

EASY RECIPES
FOR EVERYDAY
GATHERINGS

IN
GOOD
COMPANY

CORBIN TOMASZESKI

with Karen Geier

Figure .1
Vancouver / Berkeley

To Char for your
unconditional support
and love. And to Bennett,
Brodie, and Tate who will
always be my constant
source of inspiration.

Cataloguing data available from Library and Archives Canada
ISBN 978-1-77327-000-5 (hbk.)

Design by Natalie Olsen
Photography by Christian Lalonde, Photoluxstudio.com/
commercial (except page 198, photographs by Laura Takahashi)
Food styling by Noah Witenoff and Corbin Tomaszeski
Prop styling by Jennifer Evans

Editing by Michelle Meade
Copy editing by Laura Brown
Proofreading by Ruth Wilson
Indexing by Iva Cheung

Printed and bound in China by C&C Offset Printing Co., Ltd.
Distributed in the U.S. by Publishers Group West

Figure 1 Publishing Inc.
Vancouver BC Canada
www.figure1publishing.com

Recipe Notes
Butter should always be unsalted.
Eggs, vegetables, and fruits are assumed to be medium sized,
unless stated otherwise.
Milk is always 2%.
Greek yogurt is always fat-free.
Herbs are fresh unless stated otherwise.

Chef Corbin Tomaszeski would like to thank KitchenAid for
their generous support of the book:

KitchenAid

CONTENTS

RECIPE LIST

MY MOTHER'S COOKBOOK

Growing up, I remember my mother's cookbook vividly. It had a coiled spine on it. It was frayed, some of the corners were worn down, and others were stained with a patina of regular use. It had notes scrawled on the pages. It wasn't very big on its own, but if you included the stuffed-in sheets and recipe cutouts from newspapers and magazines, it was a pretty hefty tome. I would flip to certain recipes without looking: the most used ones bore evidence of spills, dustings of flour, and imprints of the water glass sometimes used to hold the page down.

That memory has always guided my vision for creating my own cookbook. I own hundreds of cookbooks in every conceivable cuisine, but the ones that I refer to most, that I use to feed my own family, bear closer resemblance to my mother's cookbook with its sticky, crinkled pages that gave up the faint whiff of spice when opened to particular recipes. I refer to these books as my "all 'rounders."

Coffee-table cookbooks are often admired for their lush photography and lengthy recipes, and I should know, as I own dozens. I wanted this cookbook to be more accessible, with approachable recipes for cooks of any skill level. Formal kitchen training shouldn't be a prerequisite for cooking delicious meals. I truly believe anyone can cook and entertain with a little guidance.

In Good Company is a combination of recipes collected from my Polish grandmother, Baba, my mother's farmhouse staples, the various stages of my culinary career, and what my wife, Charlene, and I cook for our three boys: Bennett, Brodie, and Tate. I am a strong believer that we communicate through food and by sharing traditions, and that these acts establish a greater connection with each other.

Much like the dishes from my mother's cookbook, the recipes here are designed to be shared with friends and family around a communal table. For me, the unbridled joy of preparing delicious food for those you love is second to none. I hope the food and stories from my life touch yours and remind you that food is as much about the moment and the company as it is about the ingredients. I hope that this book becomes your "all 'rounder," stained and crinkled from daily use. I hope you store your own cutouts in it because it's the first place you look in the kitchen. It would be the highest compliment I could receive.

Chef Corbin

EXPRESSIONS OF LOVE

My first food memory is definitely not a glamorous one: standing on top of phone books, peering into what seemed like cauldrons of bubbling food. The smell was intoxicating. I always wanted to know how my mother transformed our garden produce into amazing dinners every night.

The beets we pulled from the soil and the eggs we gathered from the coop would magically become part of a family meal later that night. Regardless of how tough our day was at school or on the farm, when it was time for dinner, we all sat down, enjoyed the food, and had family time. I learned to respect ingredients and to appreciate the most important part of meals—gathering with loved ones for quality time.

On weekends, we visited Baba with empty stomachs because we knew she'd stuff us to the gills with Polish delicacies. Regardless of what was happening in our lives, no matter the tumult, the pierogi and borscht were always there. Baba used to take it as a personal insult if we didn't clean our plates, but that rarely happened. She would say, "you no be eat at Baba's house, you go home." Her stern tone and thick Polish accent sent the message loud and clear: we had to eat. Those meals spent with Baba were treasured moments in time.

My mother saw that I was interested in cooking from an early age and put me to work in the kitchen. I was excited by my "promotion" because I was closer to the food (and the magic) and further away from the scraped knees and dirty fingernails of the farm.

Filled with six kids who all worked on the farm, our house went through a massive amount of potatoes, and peeling them became my number one job. I quickly learned that cooking can be extremely hard work, but if I improved my technique and peeled the potatoes faster, I was likelier to learn something else from my mother that day: whether it was making a pie crust, searing meat for a stew, seasoning a soup, or discovering any number of secrets she kept in her back pocket.

Those formative experiences laid the groundwork for my career as a chef. They taught me the essentials of turning real, fresh, close-to-the-source ingredients into delicious meals and the meaning of the dining experience: at its heart, it's about the time spent with important people in your life.

As someone who learned to cook by feel and by sense, I found my French culinary training to be a transformative experience. The discipline, technique, and higher level of complexity helped me better understand the process of food and of making offcuts into masterful dishes. It made me more appreciative of my experiences on the farm and advanced my repertoire by building on my mother's home cooking (which efficiently used everything we grew and raised). Culinary traditions are rooted in meticulous technique, but can be applied across myriad cuisines so you communicate with diners in new ways. Through this cooking "boot camp," I learned to never stop experimenting.

You need to love food in order to endure the backbreaking labor on a farm or the long days in a professional kitchen. The hours are grueling, the last-minute changes to menus are frequent, and the pressure is constant—but I wouldn't give up working in a kitchen for the world. I am blessed to be doing what I love every day, surrounded by non-conformists—that colorful cast of characters in and out of that kitchen—who share my love for food, who are passionate about unique ingredients, and who value the process as much as the end result. For some of us, this is an opportunity to create connections with food and people. For many of us, this is home.

Every day, Charlene and I teach our boys that food is a universal expression of love. Despite my travels, my food education, my experience with different cuisines and dietary concerns, food, for me, has always returned to the experience of being around a warm, loving table. My sons will enjoy the occasional take-out meals, but they've been taught that the dining experience is infinitely better when we choose the ingredients and create and prepare a meal together. They now have an interest in food provenance, they've learned how to amp-up flavor in dishes, and they are perfecting techniques along the way. They are discovering the values in creating a dish from scratch and then reaping the benefits of their hard work at the table.

If you take away one piece of advice from this book, let it be this: the moment of serving your dish and experiencing food with guests is more important than breaking a plate, misreading a recipe, or any number of goofs you make along the way. I'll show you how to improve your skills, but always with that end goal in mind: a positive food experience with people you care about.

In Good Company features a collection of my personal favorites: recipes that I have shared with friends, family, and customers over the years. Recipes such as Ploughman's Lunch (page 108) and Chicken and Dumpling Soup (page 80) evoke fond memories of a bygone era, while recipes such as Hazelnut S'more and Banana Pancakes (page 33)

and Fennel and Pistachio Crusted Lamb Rack (page 131) will be part of new experiences that will be remembered by a new generation.

Creativity is one my favorite aspects of cooking—experimenting with flavors and making new discoveries out of the successes (and failures). For this reason, I've included ideas for building your own recipes: from salad dressings (page 60) to Blood Mary or Caesar bars (page 188).

However, as a working chef, husband, and father of three with a hectic schedule, there are times when I want to prepare a fuss-free but still healthy and nutritious dinner. My "Time Crunch" recipes are designed exactly for those busy days when I need to execute a quick, tasty, and delicious meal that can be prepared in less than an hour. Best of all, these recipes allow me to spend more time with Char and the boys at the table.

Food is a conduit to sharing our lives, and Easy Entertaining offers tips for creating stress-free gatherings that will hopefully inspire you to bring friends and family together year-round. For 30 years, everyone—colleagues, friends, and family—has been calling me Chef Corbin. Traditionally, this honorific "chef" title was reserved to represent those with the highest experience and authority in the profession; however, in this case, it is more of a nickname that's free of formality and borne out of ease and familiarity by peers (and probably a bit of uncertainty in the pronunciation of my surname). For me, the moniker is an affirmation of my career origins—from my humble upbringing on an Albertan farm—and a constant reminder that food is always where the heart is, at work and at home. Let me show you how to think more like a chef, so you can spend more time connecting with your loved ones.

EASY ENTERTAINING

I love nothing more than entertaining and making people feel loved and cared for—it's the ultimate motivation behind why I became a chef. With years of experience behind me, and over 150 dinner parties critiqued on my show *Dinner Party Wars,* I've discovered how to plan and execute affairs with minimal effort and maximum impact.

Entertaining is about bringing friends and/or family together, possibly commemorating an occasion, and establishing connections around a table. Simplify your work and prepare things you know. This is not the time to test a new menu—you will shed tears in the process. (Trust me on this one, I know from experience.) Also, learn to divide and conquer: working together as a team with your partner or family members will relieve some of that self-imposed pressure, and they are often eager to help.

The number of guests and the formality of an occasion will often dictate the serving style for a large group. Plated servings, where the cook assembles dishes in the kitchen and serves individual courses to the guests, are best for more intimate and formal gatherings. Family style, where food is on the table and guests serve themselves and the dishes are often simple, rustic, and bountiful, lend to a relaxed, convivial, and familial atmosphere. Buffet style, where food is set up at one or multiple stations and guests can help themselves, is best suited for large groups between 6 and 10. For this style, I recommend setting up a station with stacked plates and restaurant style roll-ups—where utensils are wrapped in napkins—so guests have everything they need.

Above all, a gathering should be fuss-free so you can enjoy it as much as your guests. **Let's make your parties easy to plan and hard to forget.**

Wine and Beer A 750-ml bottle of wine holds five glasses. The general consumption rule for a party is that people will have two drinks in the first hour and then one drink per hour onwards.

People drink white wine more often than red, so even if you're pairing your wine, you will want to buy more white than red. If you're buying five bottles of wine total, for instance, consider getting three white and two red.

Have a wide variety of light to dark beers on hand as well, and always chill beers ahead of time. To save on budget and keep it local, consider buying growlers (64-fl-oz jugs) or individual bottles of craft beer from nearby breweries.

Wine Pairing The rule that white wine should be consumed with chicken and fish and red wine with meat is outdated and no longer applicable. Instead, consider these two things: weight and dominance.

A heavy-bodied red (Rioja, Chianti, or Malbec) may overpower salmon, but a light-bodied red such as a Pinot Noir makes a nice complement to this fish.

The term "dominance" refers to the leading notes, flavors, and/or aromatics in the wines. The strong flavor of an oaky Chardonnay pairs well with lightly cooked fish, creamy risottos, or pastas, while delicate ingredients such as shellfish are better accompanied by a light and slightly citrusy Sauvignon Blanc or Pinot Gris.

How to Read Recipes Chefs look at the overall time and number of steps to prep each dish in order to determine how the jobs can be broken down into smaller tasks, and how many can be completed ahead of time.

Reading recipes a few times in advance and making note of any nonnegotiable steps (like marinating meat overnight) can help ensure a smooth operation on the day of your event.

Make a list of ingredients to buy rather than what is available on-hand and add the quantities needed so you can shop more effectively.

How to Plan Dinners The most important thing to determine is the amount of time you'll need to assemble and cook your meal on the big day. As a chef, I will prepare multiple lists: a list of things to buy, listed by when in advance it needs to be bought (for instance, salad greens and fish should be purchased closer to the day, where nonperishable items can be bought a week or more ahead of time to minimize last-minute prep work); a list of the dishes, pots, pans, and gear needed for each recipe; and a list for advanced preparations and when they need to be done. These lists will keep you organized and on top of everything.

How to Shop With the notable exception of seafood, I strongly advise you shop at least a day before your party. If you do not, you may send the rest of your day into a tailspin.

Shopping in advance also breaks up the task into manageable trips and builds in contingencies for hard-to-find ingredients. You can rethink the recipe or work around the missing ingredient.

Table Setting Unless you want people drinking each other's wine or using each other's butter knives, tradition is the best place to start. You'll notice with classic restaurant service, waiters "serve from the left, take away from the right." For this reason, glasses should be kept on the left side of the place setting. Set your table like a restaurant sets its table, with a small fork (salad/appetizer), and big fork, knife, and spoon (soup or dessert).

Some people use larger service plates—known as liners or chargers—throughout the meal as a base under the appetizer, soup, and entrée, but these can be cumbersome and I find them unnecessary. They may look good in magazines, but they only add to the washing.

I recommend linen or uncoated cotton for napkins —anything else won't do the job of cleaning your face.

Always put out pitchers of still and sparkling water for people who want a respite from alcohol. (Plus, you never know when you might need it for stains.)

Teaching kids how to set a table is a simple task that is easy to master and keeps them occupied while you're busy doing other things. Start with plates and cutlery, and when they're older, add in the glasses.

Unless your kids are particularly unruly, I don't recommend the "kiddie table" concept. Kids will learn how to conduct themselves by example when sitting at a dinner table with adults. It's a good educational opportunity to show them how to use napkins, ask each other to pass items, or simply carry on conversations.

A Simple Plan

Establish your budget and stick to it. Before you decide on the menu, it's useful to ask yourself what you're willing to spend. This helps you manage your expenditure and allows you to create your menu accordingly.

Know your audience. As a host, you want to be sure your guests are comfortable with the food and environment. Ask yourself what they enjoy eating and if they have any dietary restrictions.

Cook what you know. When the pressure is on, simplicity is the key to success.

Prepare as much as possible in advance. The various elements can often be made in stages and ahead of time.

Taste everything. Taste it while cooking and before serving to make sure it's at its best.

Create ambiance. Lighting, music, temperature, and decorations—such as flowers, centerpieces, or candles—all contribute to atmosphere.

Delegate work if needed. Hiring, bartenders, servers, etc. can relieve the pressure and let you enjoy your own party.

Prepare the meal and drinks to suit the number of guests. You should have an idea of the number of guests, and have enough for them to eat and drink (see Wine and Beer, page 16). You don't want guests holding back, or worse, you running out.

Location, location, location. Will guests be comfortable? If you plan a party outside, what's the contingency if the weather is terrible? Some might opt for a canopy or propane heater. Charlene will often lay shawls or throws on the back of chairs.

If you do a buffet, make sure people can sit and eat. Don't serve anything that requires a knife and fork if guests are expected to stand.

Be sure everyone is in view. Don't ever put anything on a table that obscures the guests' vision.

Never put out scented candles. Avoid putting something in a room that detracts from the sensory experience of a meal or offends guests with sensitivities to certain smells.

Enjoy yourself. As host, you've prepared the food, set the tables with plates and cutlery, and offered a drink to your guests, but you also need to find the time to relax and have some fun.

MENUS

DATE NIGHT

A romantic meal is more about sentiment and gesture and less about the logistics (and possible pitfalls) of cooking. This elegant menu shows someone that you care without ruining the moment with worry or close timing.

SIMPLE DINNER PARTY

If you're new to entertaining and/or cooking, this varied menu—with its array of color, taste, and texture—is for you. The lentils and most of the crème brûlée can be prepared in advance, you can set and forget the main dish, and the final details can be finished at the time of serving.

SUNDAY SUPPER

Sunday suppers are about togetherness, so to keep things simple, my menus are often informed by seasonal ingredients. This menu comprises my "greatest hits" of comfort food and can even be served buffet style.

VEGETARIAN

The flexitarian diet—limiting meat intake to occasional servings—is becoming increasingly popular. When you prepare meat-free dishes, consider textures as well as flavors so you can leave guests equally satisfied.

BRUNCH

Set this up in buffet style: rolling up the cutlery and setting up a stack of plates at the end for maximum efficiency. I recommend serving this with bubbles or Caesars.

THE PERFECT HOLIDAY PARTY

Holiday parties are often the hardest to plan because we put so much pressure on ourselves to create a spectacular feast and Instagram-worthy presentations. Don't overthink it—most people are content with a few glasses of festive cheer.

COCKTAIL PARTY

When budgeting for a cocktail party, plan on eight pieces of finger foods per person. This helps you visualize and plan how many dishes, and how many batches of each dish, you will have to make. Soup shots are often served in tall shot glasses, which can be enjoyed without utensils.

BIG GAME

This requires the least formal dining style, and it's the only time I ever use paper plates. For sake of ease, consider putting cutlery in cups next to the plates and let people fix their own dishes, buffet style. And always put out multiple napkin stations.

BACKYARD FEAST

These dishes can either be prepared ahead or cooked on a grill, making this an ideal menu for large gatherings.

One-Bite Hors d'Oeuvres *page 52*
Summer Stack *page 61*
Lemon and Mushroom Risotto *page 154*
Spiced Chocolate Molten Cake *page 180*

Pairing: Raspberry and Mint Champagne Charger
page 192

Thai Coconut and Beer Mussels *page 46*
Spinach, Prosciutto, and Sun-Dried Tomato Salad Rolls *page 72*
Osso Buco with Gremolata *page 112*
Braised Puy Lentils *page 162*
Ginger Crème Brûlée *page 183*

Pairing: Red wine such as Chianti or white wine such as Riesling

Baba's Pierogi *page 50*
Grandma Mollison's Beet Salad *page 64*
Spatchcock Chicken of your choice *page 116*
Allspice, Cumin, and Chili Pan-Roasted Brussels Sprouts *page 147*
Stone-Fruit Crumble of your choice *page 178*

Pairing: Variety of chilled light beers and ciders

Roasted Red Pepper and Sweet Potato Soup with Halloumi Cheese *page 87*
Roasted Cauliflower Couscous *page 156*
Jicama, Radish, and Kale Superfood Salad *page 59*
Strawberry Tarte Tatin *page 175*

Pairing: Pimm's Pitcher
page 190

Farmhouse Bubble and Squeak with Smoked Salmon *page 43*
Breakfast Pizza *page 28*
Zucchini and Quinoa Muffins *page 27*
Candied Bacon *page 197*
Welsh Rarebit Bites with Blue Cheese and Onion Jam *page 53*

Pairing: Balsamic and Peppered Strawberry Champagne Charger
page 192

Chana Fritters *page 49*
Roasted Red Pepper and Sweet Potato Soup with Grilled Halloumi *page 87*
Fennel and Pistachio Crusted Lamb Rack *page 131*
Candied Beets with Maple Syrup and Chives *page 137*
Banana and Dark Chocolate Bread Pudding with Crème Anglaise *page 172*

Pairing: Christmas Party White Sangria
page 193

One-Bite Hors d'Oeuvres *page 52*
Four Season Tartines *page 98*
Ploughman's Lunch *page 108*
Mint Pea Soup shots *page 88*
Just-Like-Mom's Pudding served in ramekins or mason jars *page 173*

Pairing: Watermelon Moscow Mules
page 190

Grilled Jerk Wings *page 44*
CT Burgers/Sliders with Onion Jam *page 102*
Chicken Hand Pies *page 104*
Carole's Famous Carrot Cake *page 170*

Pairing: Buckets of beers and ciders

Pancetta-Wrapped Peaches with Rosemary *page 54*
Gazpacho with Avocado and Lime *page 82*
Grilled Watermelon with Feta, Olives, Onion, and Basil *page 63*
Cedar-Planked Pork Tenderloin with Pineapple and Onion Relish *page 121*
Cauliflower and Carrot Slaw with Honey-Curry Vinaigrette *page 70*

Pairing: Bloody Mary and Caesar Bar
page 188

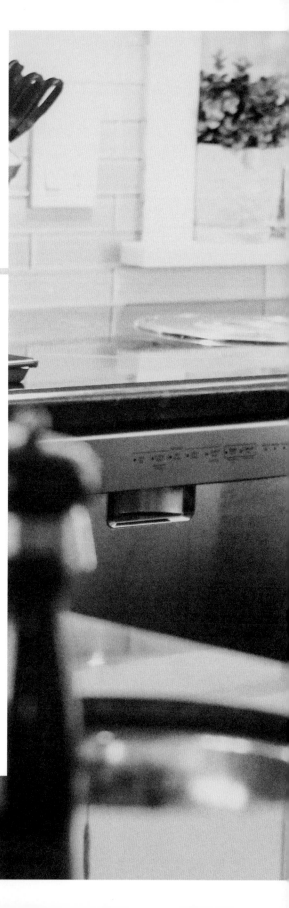

START
YOUR
DAY

Growing up on an Albertan farm, breakfast was all about sustenance—consuming as many calories as possible to get through long work and school days. These days, life is busier than ever. During the week when the alarm wakes us up at the crack of dawn, Char and I scramble to get the boys clothed, fed, and prepared for the day. We are often at the mercy of preschoolers who don't necessarily have a sense of (our) schedule, so it's important we eat nutritious breakfasts to fight fatigue and provide us with healthy, slow-burning energy to keep us going for hours. We often rely on weekday standbys such as French toast page 32, prebaked muffins page 27, and oatmeal page 34.

In contrast to our intense weekday schedule, our weekends are far more relaxed. The commitments are less, the boys sleep in, and the mornings seem almost still. When the boys eventually wake up, we make our way to the kitchen and happily while away the time by preparing a meal. I relish this quality time together: the kids exercise their creativity by adding their favorite ingredients to any given dish (the key is to start small and build) and take pride and ownership of their creations.

When Bennett was about four years old, he would help mix the pancake batter and crack eggs. Now, the boys work together to put their stamp on morning treats such as Hazelnut S'more and Banana Pancakes page 33 or Breakfast Pizza page 28. As you can see, some of the best creations were born out of these occasions, and I try not to take these seemingly ordinary moments for granted.

Breakfast Salad

One of the challenges of serving brunch to well-heeled clients is that I am constantly asked for newer, more innovative dishes. (You have to make sure that customers still want to try on the dresses after eating.) This breakfast salad that I made at the high-fashion retailer Holt Renfrew was a smash success. I had cooks prepping greens as fast as the orders were coming in. If you serve this salad at your next brunch, people will think you're a genius in the kitchen.

Preheat the oven to 200°F.

To make the salad, in a large bowl, combine all ingredients and toss to mix. Set aside.

To make the potato pancakes, combine potatoes and onions in a food processor and pulse for 30 seconds, or until smooth. Transfer mixture to a fine-mesh sieve set over a bowl and strain for 4–5 minutes. Carefully pour out the strained liquid from the bowl, keeping the potato starch that has settled at the bottom. (The starch will bind the potato pancakes.)

Add potato and onion mixture to the bowl of potato starch. Add egg, bacon, scallion, flour, and salt and pepper and mix well.

In a large cast-iron skillet over medium-high heat, heat oil. Spoon mixture into skillet in 4 equal-sized pancakes (about ¾ cup each). Gently flatten pancakes to a 3-inch diameter and cook for 4–5 minutes. Flip and cook for another 4–5 minutes, until golden and crispy. Remove from heat and place onto an ovenproof plate in the oven to keep warm until ready to serve.

To make eggs sunny-side up, melt butter in a nonstick skillet over medium heat. Crack eggs into the skillet and cook for 1–2 minutes, until egg whites are set. Season with salt and pepper.

To serve, put 1 pancake on each plate and top with an egg and salad.

VARIATION:

1 Breakfast Salad 2 Replace the sunny-side up eggs with poached eggs (page 36). Replace the bacon with crumbled pork breakfast sausage.

Serves 4

Salad
2 cups mixed greens
1 orange, peeled and segmented
1 tsp extra virgin olive oil
Salt and pepper, to taste

Potato pancakes
1 large russet potato, peeled and chopped
3 Tbsp chopped onion
1 small egg
¼ cup cooked chopped bacon
1 scallion, thinly sliced
3 Tbsp all-purpose flour
Salt and pepper, to taste
1 Tbsp vegetable oil

Eggs
1 Tbsp butter
4 eggs
Salt and pepper, to taste

Zucchini and Quinoa Muffins

Winter weekends usually start well before 6 a.m. for our family. We often need a breakfast that can be eaten in a moving car on our way to a hockey game. As a healthy alternative to cake-based muffins, this simple, on-the-go version maximizes nutrition. It's a slow-energy-release breakfast option that keeps you full and fueled longer.

In a small saucepan over high heat, bring 1 cup of water to a boil. Add quinoa and reduce the heat to low. Cover and cook for 15–20 minutes, until water is completely absorbed. You should have 1 cup of cooked quinoa.

Preheat the oven to 350°F. Using cooking spray, lightly grease an eight-cavity mini loaf pan with 2 × 4-inch compartments.

In a large bowl, combine flour, brown sugar, cinnamon, nutmeg, baking powder, and salt and mix well.

In a small bowl, whisk together eggs, milk, sour cream, melted butter, and vanilla extract. Add wet mixture to the bowl of dry ingredients and stir gently until combined. Fold in zucchini, quinoa, and raisins (or other dried fruit).

Evenly divide batter into the prepared muffin pan and bake for 25–30 minutes, or until a toothpick inserted into the center of a muffin comes out clean. Remove from the oven and cool for 10 minutes. Remove cooled muffins from pan and place on a wire baking rack to cool completely.

Top each muffin with softened cream cheese, if using. Serve with a side of fresh fruit or small bowl of yogurt.

Serves 4 (makes 8)

⅓ cup quinoa
3 cups all-purpose flour
⅔ cup packed brown sugar
1½ tsp ground cinnamon
¼ tsp ground nutmeg
1½ tsp baking powder
½ tsp salt
2 eggs
¾ cup milk
¼ cup sour cream
3½ Tbsp melted butter
1 tsp vanilla extract
1½ cups coarsely grated zucchini, water pressed out
½ cup raisins, dried cranberries, or chopped dried apricots, rinsed
Cream cheese, softened, to serve (optional)
Fresh fruit or yogurt, to serve

Breakfast Pizza

Pizza is a favorite dinner for many, including my three sons, but there's something to be said about having leftover pizza for breakfast. And this winner combines the pizza concept with bacon and eggs for a thoroughly indulgent and hearty breakfast treat. If you're making this dish for a party or a larger crew, put out options for toppings and let your guests experiment—food often tastes better when a little fun is added to the equation.

Serves 4

1-lb bag raw store-bought pizza
    dough, room temperature
All-purpose flour, for dusting
¼ cup cornmeal
1 Tbsp butter
5 eggs, beaten
Salt and pepper, to taste
1 cup softened cream cheese
1 cup cooked chopped bacon
1 large tomato, chopped (1 cup)
1 cup shredded cheddar cheese
1 scallion, thinly sliced
¼ cup torn basil

Preheat the oven to 450°F.

Lightly dust pizza dough and a clean work surface with flour. Roll out dough into a 12-inch disk.

Sprinkle a 14-inch round pizza pan (or baking sheet) with cornmeal and place pizza dough on top. Using a fork, pierce dough to prevent it from bubbling when baking. Bake for 8 minutes, or until cooked through and golden.

Meanwhile, prepare the scrambled eggs. In a nonstick skillet over medium-high heat, melt butter. Add eggs and stir gently for 5 minutes to scramble. Season with salt and pepper and set aside.

Spread cream cheese over baked dough and top with scrambled eggs. Sprinkle bacon, tomatoes, cheddar cheese, and scallions overtop. Bake for another 3–5 minutes, or until the cheese melts.

Cut into 8 slices, sprinkle basil overtop and serve.

VARIATIONS:

1 **Veggie Pizza** Replace the bacon with 1 red bell pepper, seeded and chopped. Replace the cheddar cheese with ¾ cup crumbled feta cheese.

2 **Lox and Cheese** Replace the bacon with 5 large slices of smoked salmon. Replace the basil with ¼ cup dill.

Breakfast Tostadas
with Black Beans and Pico de Gallo

Tostadas may have gotten their start in small taquerias in Mexico, but they have taken the brunch scene by storm. Tostadas are crisp tortilla bases topped with everything you might find in a taco. And as a great vegetarian option for breakfast, I've never seen a kid pass on this dish.

To make the black bean purée, in a medium bowl, combine all ingredients. Using a potato masher, mash until smooth and creamy. Set aside.

To make the pico de gallo, in a small bowl, combine all ingredients and mix well.

To make the tostadas, in a 10-inch cast-iron skillet over medium-high heat, heat oil. Carefully add 1 tortilla and fry for 30 seconds. Flip and fry for another 30 seconds until crispy and golden in color. Transfer tortilla to a plate lined with paper towels. Repeat with the remaining tortillas.

Drain excess oil from skillet and return to stove. Add butter and melt over medium-high heat. Crack eggs into skillet and cook for 1–2 minutes, until egg whites are set, sunny-side up.

To assemble, spread black bean purée on fried tortillas. Top each with a fried egg and a spoonful of pico de gallo. Season with salt and pepper. Garnish with cilantro and serve with a lime wedge.

VARIATION:

1 **Breakfast Tostadas with Bacon, Black Beans, and Pico de Gallo** Sprinkle ½ cup of your favorite grated cheese overtop and add ½ cup crispy bacon or crumbled sausage.

Serves 4

Black bean purée
1½ cups cooked black beans, warm
1 scallion, finely chopped
Juice and zest of 1 lime
½ tsp chili powder
½ tsp ground cumin
¼ tsp kosher salt
Coarsely ground black pepper

Pico de gallo
2 small tomatoes, chopped
    (about ¼ cup)
½ small onion, finely chopped
    (about ¼ cup)
½ jalapeno, finely chopped
1 Tbsp lime juice
¼ tsp kosher salt

Tostadas
½ cup canola or vegetable oil
4 (5½-inch) corn tortillas
1 tsp butter
4 large eggs
Salt and pepper, to taste
½ cup chopped cilantro
1 lime, cut into quarters, to serve

Mini Dutch Babies
with Stewed Raspberries

Serves 4

Stewed raspberries
2 cups fresh raspberries or any
    seasonal berries, rinsed and
    dried
1 Tbsp granulated sugar
1 Tbsp orange zest

Dutch babies
¼ cup (½ stick) butter, melted
5 eggs, room temperature
1 cup milk
1 cup all-purpose flour
2 Tbsp granulated sugar
1 tsp vanilla extract
Pinch of salt
Mint leaves, to garnish

Dutch babies, or breakfast popovers, are a thing of beauty: light, crispy, and tender all at once, and a great carrier for sweet or savory fillings and toppings. Made from a batter poured into a screaming-hot pan, they puff up and brown (a bit like Yorkshire puddings).

Chefs can pull out a lot of tricks for breakfast and brunch services. Dutch babies are deceptively easy to make and will convince your guests that you're a magician in the kitchen. To prepare this recipe for a group, make the batter in advance so cooking is all you need to do at the time of serving.

To make the stewed raspberries, in a small saucepan over medium heat, combine all ingredients and bring to a boil. Reduce heat to low, stir and cook for another 2 minutes. Remove from heat and set aside.

To make the Dutch babies, preheat the oven to 425°F. Pour a teaspoon of melted butter into each cup of a 12-cup muffin pan and place in the oven.

In a blender, combine eggs, milk, flour, sugar, vanilla, and salt. Cover and blend for 1½ minutes, until the batter is well mixed and smooth.

Remove the muffin pan from the oven. Evenly divide the batter among the cups and bake for 20 minutes, or until puffed up and golden.

Place 3 Dutch babies each onto 4 plates and serve warm with stewed raspberries. Garnish with mint leaves.

Waffle Iron French Toast

A waffle iron may only be used a handful of times each year, but don't overlook it! I often use one at the hotel to introduce some texture to ingredients. In this case, I marry two classic breakfast concepts— French toast and waffles—and transform them into an elegant morning treat. If you're planning for a crowd, they can be made in advance and kept in a warm oven on a low-temperature setting.

Preheat a waffle iron to 360°F. Preheat oven to 200°F.

In a medium bowl, whisk eggs for 2 minutes, until frothy. Add milk (or cream), sugar, vanilla, cinnamon, nutmeg, and salt and mix well.

Brush both sides of the waffle iron with melted butter. Dip 1 slice of bread into egg mixture, place onto waffle iron, and close. Cook for 3–4 minutes, until crispy and golden. Place cooked slice onto an ovenproof plate in the oven to keep warm. Repeat for remaining slices.

Place 2 slices of French toast each onto 4 plates. Drizzle with maple syrup and dust with icing sugar. Serve with a dollop of yogurt and garnish with a mint leaf.

VARIATION:

1 Waffle Iron Crêpe Suzette Replace the serving ingredients with a Crêpe Suzette sauce. In a small saucepan, combine the juice of 2 oranges, ½ cup granulated sugar, 3 Tbsp Grand Marnier, and a pinch of salt and bring to a boil. Reduce heat to low and cook for another 5 minutes. Remove from heat and stir in 3 Tbsp cold butter. Drizzle over waffles and serve.

Serves 4

6 eggs
2 cups milk or half-and-half (10%) cream
1½ Tbsp brown sugar
2 tsp vanilla extract
1 tsp ground cinnamon
¼ tsp ground nutmeg
Pinch of salt
2 Tbsp melted butter, for greasing
8 (1-inch-thick) slices day-old brioche or challah, crusts removed

To serve
½ cup pure maple syrup
Icing sugar, for dusting
Mint leaves, to garnish
Plain yogurt

Hazelnut S'more and Banana Pancakes

Serves 4
(about 8 large pancakes)

1¼ cups milk
1 large egg, beaten
1 tsp vanilla extract
1 small overripe banana, mashed
¾ cup all-purpose flour
¼ cup graham cracker crumbs
2 tsp baking powder
½ tsp salt
1 Tbsp granulated sugar
¼ cup Nutella
8 large marshmallows, halved
Pure maple syrup, to serve

My sons first learned how to cook by making pancakes. At first, most of that time was spent trying to eat the batter, but eventually, they became excited about the process: making different shapes and flipping the pancakes when the bubbles begin to pop or burst. Over the years, more ingredients were added to the dish (at their request), which is how we ended up with this child-friendly, carnival-level breakfast dish. Be warned, it's not meant for anyone looking to shed a few pounds.

In a large bowl, combine milk, egg, vanilla, and banana and whisk until smooth.

In a medium bowl, combine flour, graham cracker crumbs, baking powder, salt, and sugar and mix well. Add flour mixture to liquid mixture and stir until the batter is smooth. Set aside.

Heat a nonstick griddle or skillet over medium-high heat. Using a ¼-cup measuring cup, ladle batter onto the griddle and cook for 1–2 minutes. Flip and cook for another 1–2 minutes, or until golden.

Spread ½ Tbsp of Nutella onto each pancake. Top 1 pancake with 4 marshmallow halves. Repeat with 3 more pancakes. Place remaining 4 pancakes, Nutella-side down, on top of the marshmallow topped ones and serve with a side of maple syrup.

VARIATIONS:

1 Peanut Butter, Chocolate Chip, and Banana Pancakes
Replace Nutella with peanut butter and add ¼ cup chocolate chips to the batter.

2 Nut-Free Pancakes Replace the Nutella with softened cream cheese.

Brûléed Blueberry Oatmeal

Serves 4

3½ cups water
¼ tsp salt
2 cups rolled oats
½ cup toasted walnuts
1 cup blueberries
2 Tbsp granulated sugar
Milk or cream, to serve

It sounds clichéd, but my mother started every morning with a dedicated pot of oatmeal. Every time I cook oatmeal, I'm brought back to my childhood when the smell wafted up the stairs as we stumbled around on cold winter mornings.

One of the biggest challenges of cooking for private events is creating unique and special dishes inspired by familiarity. A riff on a classic combination, this indulgent oatmeal is a good example of elevating ordinary ingredients by adding a few choice techniques and presenting them in ramekins.

Preheat the broiler to high heat.

In a medium saucepan over high heat, combine water and salt and bring to a boil. Add rolled oats and stir gently. Reduce heat to medium-low and simmer, uncovered, for 5–6 minutes. Remove from heat. Stir in toasted walnuts.

Evenly divide oatmeal among 4 (1-cup) ramekins. Top with blueberries and sprinkle 1½ tsp sugar into each ramekin.

Place the ramekins on a large baking sheet and broil for 1 minute, or until the sugar melts and caramelizes.

Serve warm with milk or cream.

VARIATIONS:

1. **Brûléed Banana and Dried Cranberry Oatmeal** Replace the blueberries with 1 large banana, thinly sliced. Replace the walnuts with dried cranberries.

2. **Brûléed Peach and Toasted Almond Oatmeal** Replace the blueberries with 2 large peaches, pitted and sliced into thin wedges. Replace the walnuts with toasted almonds.

Poached Eggs, Smashed Avocado, and Vine-Ripened Tomatoes on Toast

Serves 4

8 cups water
2 Tbsp white vinegar
8 eggs
4 (½-inch-thick) slices sourdough
    bread
2 ripened avocados, pitted, peeled
    and smashed with a fork
2 cups arugula
1 cup peeled and thinly sliced
    English cucumber
¼ small red onion, thinly sliced
2 cups cherry tomatoes, halved
4 tsp extra virgin olive oil, plus
    more for drizzling
Salt and pepper, to taste
Basil leaves, to garnish
Poached shrimp or smoked
    salmon, to serve (optional)

In French culinary tradition, the many folds on a chef's hat (lovingly called a "coffee filter" by cooks who feel embarrassed wearing them) symbolize the many ways to cook eggs—and a perfectly poached egg might be the height of egg cookery.

Adding vinegar to the cooking water encourages the egg proteins to set more quickly, without altering the taste. Complementary ingredients such as avocado and tomatoes are added to highlight the flavor of an egg.

In a large saucepan, combine water and vinegar. Bring to a boil over high heat. Reduce heat to medium-low and let water simmer. Crack an egg into a small bowl and carefully lower the egg into water. Repeat with 3 more eggs. Cover, turn off the heat and cook eggs for 5 minutes. Using a large slotted spoon, gently remove poached eggs and transfer to a plate. Repeat with remaining 4 eggs.

Toast the sourdough lightly on both sides. Spread the smashed avocado onto the toasted sourdough and place on a large serving platter.

In a medium bowl, combine arugula, cucumbers, onions, tomatoes, and olive oil. Toss to mix. Season with salt and pepper. Place some greens on each toast then top with 2 poached eggs. Drizzle olive oil overtop and garnish with basil. Serve with poached shrimp (or smoked salmon), if using, to create the ultimate brunch platter.

Egg White Frittata Cups

with Asparagus, Leek, and Dill

Serves 4–6

12 tulip parchment paper liners
½ Tbsp butter
1 leek, white part only, chopped
    (1½ cups)
3 small asparagus stalks, trimmed
    and sliced (½ cup)
12 egg whites
¾ cup low-fat cottage cheese
2 Tbsp chopped dill
Salt and pepper, to taste
Salad greens, to serve

Breakfast can't always be a carb fest. If you're looking for a change of pace, or you've been overdoing the holiday cheer, try lighter, healthier options for breakfast. And with a little bit of presentation finesse, in the form of herb garnishes and/or lemon zest, these cups can be served in tulip parchment paper liners for an elegant Mother's Day brunch. They are also quite portable, making them great for on-the-go breakfasts.

Preheat the oven to 375°F. Line a 12-cup muffin pan with parchment paper liners.

In a small skillet over medium-high heat, melt butter. Add leeks and cook for 4 minutes, until tender. Add asparagus and sauté for another minute. Remove from heat.

Spoon equal portions of leek-and-asparagus mixture into the prepared muffin pan.

In a large bowl, using a balloon whisk, whisk egg whites until frothy. Stir in cottage cheese and dill and season with salt and pepper.

Pour equal amounts of egg white mixture into prepared muffin pan. Bake for 20–25 minutes, or until the frittatas are firm in the center.

Serve frittatas with a side of salad greens.

VARIATION:

1 Egg White Frittata Cups with Feta, Onions, and Tomato
Replace the leek with 1½ cups chopped onions and the cottage cheese with feta cheese. Add 1 cup chopped tomatoes and replace the dill with basil or tarragon.

Baked Eggs, Chorizo, and Potato Skillet

Serves 4

3 red skin potatoes, cut into ½-inch
    dice (2½ cups)
Pinch of salt
1 Tbsp olive oil
½ lb raw chorizo sausage
½ onion, chopped (½ cup)
1 Tbsp butter
2 cloves garlic, finely chopped
2 cups chopped spinach
¼ cup chopped parsley
4 eggs
Salt and pepper, to taste
1 red bell pepper, seeded and cut
    into thin rounds
½ cup shredded Parmesan cheese
½ cup microgreens or basil
    sprouts, to garnish

This hearty one-pan dish of eggs cooked with chorizo and potato is popular morning fare for lazy weekends. Accented with peppers, parsley, and microgreens for a welcome boost of color and flavor, this recipe is bold and vibrant. My durable and reliable cast-iron skillet was handed down from my grandmother to my mother to me as a cherished heirloom—it delivers consistent heat and can withstand high temperatures without warping.

Preheat the oven to 375°F.

In a medium saucepan, combine potatoes and salt and add enough cold water to cover. Bring to a boil over high heat. Cover, reduce heat to low, and cook for 15–20 minutes, until tender. Drain and set aside to cool completely.

In a large cast-iron skillet over medium-high heat, heat oil. Add chorizo and onions and sauté for 5–6 minutes, until cooked through. Transfer mixture to a plate and set aside.

In the same skillet over medium-high heat, melt butter. Add potatoes and garlic and sauté for 5 minutes, until potatoes are crispy and golden. Return sausage to skillet, add spinach and parsley and stir until ingredients are incorporated. Remove from heat.

Using the bottom of a ladle or a wooden spoon, gently make four shallow indentations in the mixture. Carefully crack an egg into each indentation and season with salt and pepper. Arrange sliced red peppers overtop of mixture. Bake for 8–10 minutes, or until the egg whites are cooked but the yolks are still runny.

Sprinkle grated Parmesan cheese and microgreens (or basil sprouts) overtop. Serve warm.

VARIATION:

1 **Turkey, Rotini, Cherry Tomato, and Kale Skillet** Replace the chorizo sausage with ½ lb ground turkey or chicken. Replace the potatoes with 2–3 cups leftover rotini or penne pasta. Add 1 cup halved cherry tomatoes and replace the spinach with kale.

SHARE THE LOVE

Food memories are made when we have good company and great food to share. Informal family-style gatherings always seem to lend themselves to more convivial experiences and meaningful interactions. When the formality of hosting is removed from the equation, I find my time is better spent engaging with our guests and we can help ourselves to food and drink as we see fit. Small plates are nothing to scoff at.

I love the challenge of creating dishes on a whim, and small plates often lend themselves to the spontaneity.
Once, at Holt Renfrew, a request for a special order came in for Sophia Loren. I was provided a guide to her preferences, and within a matter of minutes, I presented an artfully arranged plate of figs, prosciutto, and other delights. (She said it was the best plate of figs she ever had.) And when friends come over unexpectedly (a good problem to have), I will often do a quick pantry raid and create a platter of assorted cold meats, cheese, chutneys, and crackers. Served on a rustic wooden board, it makes an impressive quick-fix presentation that's perfect for impromptu occasions.

My small plate preferences lean towards simple dishes such as Spicy Crunchy Chickpeas with Chutney and Chana Fritters page 49, Thai Coconut and Beer Mussels page 46, and Chicken Wings page 44. They may come from humble beginnings, but pair them with bold seasonings and they transform into the ultimate comfort fare. When you're looking for something slightly more elevated, the One-Bite Hors d'Oeuvres page 52 allow your guests to fill up on the dishes they like best. Some hors d'oeuvres can even be made ahead of time, which saves you a lot of work on the day of your party. Any leftovers will go fast, too. The beauty of small plates is that you can combine any number of dishes together, and it will never be wrong.

Farmhouse Bubble and Squeak
with Smoked Salmon

Serves 4

2 Tbsp butter
½ small onion, chopped
   (about ¼ cup)
1 cup shredded Brussels sprouts
3 cups mashed potatoes, room
   temperature
2 scallions, finely chopped
1 Tbsp all-purpose flour
Salt and pepper, to taste
1 Tbsp vegetable oil
3 Tbsp sour cream
4 oz smoked salmon, sliced
1 Tbsp chopped chives

When I was growing up on our farm, we'd often have a surplus of certain ingredients, notably potatoes. (We must have gone through about 50 pounds of potatoes each week.) My grandmother would prepare bubble and squeak with day-old leftover mashed potatoes, and we would add whatever we had around to enhance the flavor and nutrition of the dish. I've introduced sour cream, chopped chives, and smoked salmon to create an arguably more refined version of this family favorite.

In a skillet over medium-high heat, melt butter. Add onions and Brussels sprouts and sauté for 4 minutes, until onions are softened and translucent. Transfer mixture to large bowl.

Add mashed potatoes, scallions, and flour to bowl. Season with salt and pepper and gently toss to mix. Divide mixture into 8 and shape each into patties about 3 inches in diameter and ½-inch thick. Set aside.

In the same skillet over medium-high heat, heat oil. Add patties and cook for 4–5 minutes. Flip and cook for another 4–5 minutes, until crispy and golden.

To serve, transfer bubble and squeak to a serving platter. Place a spoonful of sour cream on each patty. Top with a ½-oz slice of smoked salmon and garnish with chopped chives.

VARIATION:

1 Bubble and Squeak with Cabbage, Pancetta, and Poached Shrimp
Replace the Brussels sprouts with shredded cabbage, then add ¾ cup chopped red bell pepper or shredded carrots and ¼ cup crispy pancetta to the potato mixture. Cook the patties in 1 Tbsp of duck or goose fat for extra flavor and top with poached shrimp.

Chicken Wings Three Ways

We're a true hockey family, and the most requested dish is always wings. But make no mistake, these are not your average bar wings. I've made every conceivable version, and here are a few of my favorites. It's worth noting that not all wings need to be fried—oven-roasted wings make a healthy and delicious alternative

Makes 12

1

Shrimp-Stuffed Chicken Wings

Shrimp stuffing
1 cup raw shrimp, peeled and deveined
2 Tbsp chopped cilantro
1 tsp chopped jalapeno
1 Tbsp grated ginger
1 clove garlic, chopped
1 tsp sesame oil
1 tsp salt
2 Tbsp vegetable oil

Chicken wings
12 deboned chicken wings, wing tip on

Preheat the oven to 400°F. Line a baking sheet with parchment paper.

To make the stuffing, in a food processor, combine shrimp, cilantro, jalapeno, ginger, garlic, sesame oil, and salt. Pulse until mixed and slightly chunky.

Using a teaspoon, stuff a spoonful of the shrimp stuffing into each chicken wing.

In a heavy-bottomed skillet over medium-high heat, heat vegetable oil. Add wings and sear until golden on all sides. Transfer wings to the prepared baking sheet and bake for 30–45 minutes, until cooked through and the internal temperature reaches 165°F. Serve.

Baked Piri Piri Wings

Piri piri rub
1¼ tsp paprika
1¼ tsp piri piri powder
½ tsp granulated sugar
½ tsp oregano leaves
½ tsp salt
¼ tsp black pepper
¼ tsp ground cinnamon
¼ tsp ground cardamom
¼ tsp ground ginger

Chicken wings
12 whole chicken wings
3 Tbsp olive oil
½ onion, finely chopped (about ½ cup)
2 cloves garlic, finely chopped
Juice of ½ lemon

To make the piri piri rub, in a small bowl, combine all ingredients and mix well. (Alternatively, combine all ingredients in a resealable jar, cover, and shake well.)

In a large bowl, combine chicken wings, olive oil, onions, garlic, and lemon juice. Mix well to completely coat the wings. Sprinkle rub over wings, cover bowl with plastic wrap, and refrigerate for 4–6 hours.

Preheat the oven to 400°F. Line a baking sheet with parchment paper.

Transfer chicken wings to the prepared baking sheet and bake for 30–45 minutes, until cooked through and the internal temperature reaches 165°F. Serve.

Grilled Jerk Wings

Jerk marinade
1 scallion, chopped
½ onion, chopped (about ½ cup)
¼ cup soy sauce
1 Tbsp grated ginger
3 Tbsp vegetable oil
2 Tbsp lemon juice
2 Tbsp HP sauce
1 large clove garlic, chopped
1 Tbsp lime juice
1 Tbsp brown sugar
½ Tbsp chopped thyme
1 tsp red pepper flakes
¼ tsp ground cloves
¼ tsp ground nutmeg
¼ tsp ground allspice

Chicken wings
12 whole chicken wings
Lemon or lime wedges, to serve

To make the jerk marinade, in a blender, combine all ingredients. Cover and blend until smooth. Place chicken wings in a large resealable plastic bag, add marinade, and refrigerate for at least 4 hours or overnight.

Preheat one side of the barbecue to 350°F.

Remove plastic bag from fridge. Place a small saucepan over medium-high heat and carefully drain marinade into saucepan. Bring to a boil. Reduce heat to medium-low and simmer for 15 minutes.

Place wings on the hot side of the grill and cook for 5 minutes on each side, basting with marinade, until browned. Move wings to heat-free side of the grill, close lid, and cook for 20 minutes, until cooked through and the internal temperature reaches 165°F. Transfer wings to a platter and serve with lemon or lime wedges.

Tip: To make in the oven, preheat the oven to 350°F. Heat a grill pan over medium-high heat. Sear wings in grill pan instead of on barbecue, and then cook in oven instead of on barbecue.

Thai Coconut and Beer Mussels

Serves 4

2 Tbsp vegetable oil
1 small onion, thinly sliced
1½ Tbsp grated ginger
2 cloves garlic, finely chopped
1 Tbsp Thai red curry paste
Pinch of red pepper flakes
1 (8-oz) can coconut milk
1 cup pale ale beer
1 Tbsp fish sauce
2 Tbsp brown sugar
3 lb mussels, scrubbed and
    debearded
Salt and pepper, to taste
2 tsp lime juice
½ cup chopped cilantro
¼ cup chopped basil
Crusty bread, to serve

Canada has so much amazing shellfish available, yet so few people actually make mussels at home. In fact, whenever I travel to Prince Edward Island (one of my favorite coastal destinations), I always make a trip out to get mussels. Not only are they cheap and delicious, they make for a quick and easy snack or dinner.

The hoppy, citrus flavor of the pale ale pairs beautifully with the rich coconut milk for a nicely balanced dish that's also complemented by the freshness of coriander and basil.

In a large 6-quart Dutch oven over medium-high heat, heat oil. Add onions, ginger, and garlic and sauté for 1–2 minutes, until fragrant.

Add curry paste and red pepper flakes and cook for another minute. Add coconut milk, beer, fish sauce, and brown sugar and stir. Bring to a boil. Reduce heat to a simmer and add mussels. Stir until mussels are coated. Cover and cook for 7–8 minutes, until mussels have opened. Remove Dutch oven from the heat and discard any unopened mussels.

Season mussels with salt and pepper and add lime juice, cilantro, and basil. Serve with large pieces of crusty bread.

VARIATION:

1 Thai Coconut Mussels with Baby Bok Choy and Jasmine Rice
Replace the beer with vegetable stock, add 2 cups chopped baby bok choy with the mussels, and serve over steamed jasmine rice.

Spicy Crunchy Chickpeas

with Chutney and Chana Fritters

My love for Indian food informed this recipe. The fritters can be made ahead of time and kept warm in a low oven until ready to serve. I created the Spicy Crunchy Chickpeas as a nutritious alternative to processed snacks—even the most discerning health fanatics eat these by the handful.

To make the spicy crunchy chickpeas, in a large bowl or container, combine chickpeas and water. Cover with plastic wrap and soak in the refrigerator overnight.

Drain, then place chickpeas in a medium saucepan and add enough water to cover. Bring to a boil over high heat and cook for 5 minutes, or until half cooked. Drain and rinse under cold water. Spread chickpeas on a large tea towel to dry.

In a heavy-bottomed pot or deep fryer, heat oil to 360°F. Gently lower dried chickpeas into the hot oil (working in batches, if necessary, to avoid overcrowding) and fry for 5–6 minutes, until golden and crispy. Using a slotted spoon, remove chickpeas and place in a shallow dish lined with paper towels. Set aside to soak up oil.

In a medium bowl, combine chickpeas, chaat (or garam) masala, and salt. Gently toss to mix. Place in small bowls.

To make the coconut-ginger chutney, combine all ingredients in a blender. Cover and blend until smooth. Set aside.

To make the chana fritters, in a heavy-bottomed pot or deep fryer, heat oil to 360°F.

In a large bowl, combine chickpea flour, cumin seeds, coriander seeds, curry powder (or garam masala), and salt and mix well. Add garlic, ginger, onions, carrots, spinach, cauliflower, and cilantro and stir to coat. Pour water into mixture and stir gently to form a thick batter.

Using a tablespoon, carefully lower heaping spoons of batter into the hot oil (working in batches, if necessary, to avoid overcrowding) and fry for 2 minutes. Flip and fry for another 2 minutes, until golden, crispy, and cooked through. Using a large slotted spoon, transfer the fritters to a plate lined with paper towels.

Serve the fritters hot, or at room temperature, with chutney and the bowls of chickpeas.

Serves 4

Spicy crunchy chickpeas
2 cups dried chickpeas
6 cups water
4 cups vegetable oil
½ tsp chaat masala or garam masala
1 tsp salt

Coconut-ginger chutney
½ cup chopped cilantro leaves and stems
1 cup chopped spinach
1½ Tbsp grated ginger
¼ cup grated unsweetened coconut
1 cup coconut milk
½ tsp red pepper flakes
1 Tbsp brown sugar

Chana fritters
4 cups vegetable oil
1¾ cups chickpea flour (or chana flour)
½ Tbsp cumin seeds
½ Tbsp ground coriander seeds
1½ tsp curry powder or garam masala
1 tsp salt
1 clove garlic, finely chopped
1 Tbsp grated ginger
½ onion, thinly sliced (½ cup)
1 carrot, shredded
1 cup spinach, chopped
½ cup chopped cauliflower
¼ cup chopped cilantro
½ cup water

Baba's Pierogi

Spending Sundays at Baba's house is one of my most formative childhood memories. Every family meal at Baba's involved pierogi and, at times, the entire kitchen would be taken over with hundreds of them. These days, my sons get involved by helping cut out the pierogi.

Line a large baking sheet with parchment paper.

To make the dough, in a large bowl, combine flour and salt and mix well. Make a large well in the center and pour in eggs, vegetable shortening, and water. Using your hands, gently pull the flour into the liquid mixture and mix until a smooth dough forms. Cover with plastic wrap and refrigerate for 20 minutes.

To make the filling, in a saucepan over medium-high heat, melt butter. Add onions and sauté for 2–4 minutes, until tender. Remove from heat and set aside to cool.

In a large bowl, combine mashed potato, onions, cottage cheese, and dill and season with salt and pepper. Mix well.

To assemble, roll out dough on a lightly floured surface to a ⅛-inch thickness. Using a 3-inch round cookie cutter or an inverted drinking glass dipped in flour, cut dough into rounds. Reroll scraps and repeat until you have 40 rounds.

Place 1 tablespoon of filling in the center of each round. Gently fold the round over to form a half-moon shape and pinch the edges. Repeat with remaining rounds.

Bring a large pot of salted water to a boil over high heat. Gently lower pierogi into the pot (working in batches, if necessary, to avoid overcrowding) and cook for 3–4 minutes, or until they rise to the surface. Using a slotted spoon, transfer pierogi to prepared baking sheet.

To serve, in large nonstick skillet over medium-high heat, melt butter. Add pierogi and fry for 2–3 minutes. Flip and cook for another 2–3 minutes, until slightly crispy and golden. Serve with chopped scallions, dill, sour cream, and caramelized onions, if using.

VARIATIONS:

 Kasha or Buckwheat Pierogi Replace the cottage cheese and dill with ½ cup cooked kasha or buckwheat.

2 **Bacon and Cheddar Pierogi** Replace the cottage cheese with ½ cup grated cheddar and ⅓ cup chopped cooked bacon.

Serves 8–10
(makes 40 pierogi)

Dough
3 cups all-purpose flour
1 tsp salt
2 eggs, beaten
½ cup vegetable shortening, melted
1 cup cold water

Potato filling
1 Tbsp butter
½ onion, finely chopped (½ cup)
1½ cups mashed potatoes
½ cup cottage cheese
1 Tbsp chopped dill
Salt and pepper, to taste

To serve
2 Tbsp butter
1 bunch scallions, chopped
Fresh dill
1 cup sour cream
1 cup Caramelized Onions
(page 196, optional)

Tip: The pierogi can be prepared in large batches and frozen. After they're boiled, arrange them on baking sheets lined with wax paper and place in the freezer. Once frozen, transfer pierogi into plastic resealable bags and keep frozen. When ready to serve, parboil the pierogi and serve with butter. Alternatively, in a skillet over medium-high heat, fry pierogi (straight from freezer) with oil and onions for 10–12 minutes, until crispy and golden brown.

One-Bite
Hors d'Oeuvres

I could write a complete book just on hors d'oeuvres (we once made 20,000 canapés for a *Vanity Fair* party). When my family and I go to our friends' cottages, we often find that the local grocers have limited stock, or worse, they're closed when we're hungry. That's when building hors d'oeuvres comes in handy.

This is a great way to teach kids about flavor pairing, and it gets everyone involved creatively. You can put together reliably good hors d'oeuvres from basic ingredients found in your cupboards or even at the smallest food shops.

Simply select a base, filling, topping, and garnish. Once you get the basic concept down, you can experiment and go wild.

Base

Toasted baguette slices, cut into 1-inch-thick rounds
English cucumbers, cut into ¼-inch-thick rounds
Baked mini puff pastry, cut into 1-inch-diameter rounds
Assorted sliced bread, cut into quarters, triangles, or squares
Assorted crisps or crackers
Mini roasted potatoes, cut into ½-inch-thick rounds

Spread

Softened goat cheese
Cream cheese
Sour cream
Mayonnaise (add fresh herbs or roasted garlic, page 196)
Olive tapenade
Hummus
Chutney
Jams or marmalades
Mustards
Vegetable or bean dips

Topping

Sliced avocado
Grilled or roasted vegetables
Cured meats or sausage
Fish and seafood (poached shrimp, cooked lobster, crabmeat, smoked fish, or grilled seafood)
Leftover grilled poultry or meat
Marinated tofu
Assorted cheese

Garnish

Fresh herbs or sprouts
Toasted seeds or nuts
Dry herbs and spices
Crispy chips or onions
Scallions
Shaved fennel or radish
Crumbled feta or blue cheese
Sliced pickles
Sliced fruit such as apples, pears, or strawberries

Welsh Rarebit Bites
with Blue Cheese and Onion Jam

This humble dish—originally made by Welsh ladies for tea breaks—was a sell-out when we put it on the high-tea menu at Holt Renfrew. When I travel along the East Coast, I love stopping into Old English neighborhood pubs, which have the best fuss-free fare. The toasted bread with melted cheese snack is a perfect example. It pairs well with beer, fills you up, and leaves you wanting more. Bonus: kids love it, and older children can learn to make it.

Line a large baking sheet with parchment paper.

To make the onion jam, in a large skillet over medium-high heat, heat oil. Add onions and sauté for 5 minutes, until softened and translucent. Add the salt, maple syrup, vinegar, and fennel seeds and stir. Reduce heat to low and cook for another 10–15 minutes, until onions are tender and sweet. Remove from heat and set aside to cool.

To make the Welsh rarebit, preheat the oven to broil.

Brush both sides of baguette slices with melted butter. Clean skillet and heat over medium heat. Add baguette slices and toast on both sides until brown and crispy. Transfer to prepared baking sheet.

In a small bowl, combine blue cheese, sour cream, and mustard and season with salt and cayenne pepper. Spread 1 tsp of onion jam onto each toast. Top with 1½ Tbsp of blue cheese mixture and broil for 3 minutes, until bubbly and golden brown. (Keep your eyes on it to prevent it from burning.)

To serve, transfer bites to a serving platter and garnish with a slice of apple (or pear) and a sprig of parsley.

VARIATION:

1 Orange and Gruyère on Toast Replace the baguette slices with day-old rye bread (fresh rye is too soft and the bread should be a little drier for best results). Replace the onion jam with orange marmalade and substitute the blue cheese with grated Gruyère or aged white cheddar. Replace the apple and parsley with cured meat or sausage.

Serves 4 (makes 12)

Onion jam
2 Tbsp vegetable oil
1 lb red onions, thinly sliced
Pinch of salt
2 Tbsp pure maple syrup
½ cup red wine vinegar
½ tsp fennel seeds

Welsh rarebit
1 small baguette, cut diagonally
    into ¾-inch-thick slices
¼ cup (½ stick) butter, melted
¾ cup crumbled blue cheese
3½ Tbsp sour cream
1 tsp grainy mustard
Salt, to taste
Pinch of cayenne pepper
12 thin slices Granny Smith apple
    or Anjou pear
12 small sprigs of parsley

Pancetta-Wrapped Peaches

with Rosemary

Makes 12

12 thin slices pancetta
2 large peaches, each cut into
    6 wedges
12 small sprigs of rosemary, about
    1½-inches long
1 Tbsp pure maple syrup
1 tsp olive oil
Coarsely ground black pepper
Green leaf salad, to serve (optional)

When I'm grilling in the summertime, I look for fresh, local, and seasonal ingredients that don't require a lot of work to taste incredible. This dish is the result of a playful experimentation of sweet and savory flavors (similar to melon and prosciutto) and aromatic herbs.

Heat a grill pan over medium heat or preheat the barbecue to 350°F

Wrap a slice of pancetta around a peach wedge and secure using a rosemary sprig. Repeat with the remaining wedges.

In a small ramekin or bowl, combine maple syrup and olive oil and mix well. Brush each wedge with mixture and place on the grill. Cook for 3–5 minutes, until pancetta is crispy on all sides.

Remove from heat. Season with pepper and serve as is or over a green leaf salad, if using.

VARIATIONS:

1 **Prosciutto-Wrapped Pineapple Bites** Replace the pancetta with prosciutto and replace the peaches with 12 pineapple wedges.

2 **Bacon-Wrapped Apricots** Replace the pancetta with bacon and the peaches with 6 apricots halved. Sprinkle a little chopped red chili overtop apricots before wrapping in bacon.

Polenta Nachos
with Sausage

Serves 4

2 cups chicken stock or water
Pinch of salt, plus more to taste
½ cup cornmeal
4 hot Italian sausage
1 Tbsp butter
¾ cup chopped parsley
1 cup crumbled Doritos Nacho
  Cheese tortilla chips
Pepper, to taste

Polenta is another word for grits. Traditionally, the two use a different size grind and corn variety, but they are both made from stone-ground corn. If you visit the southern United States, you will see hundreds of riffs on grits. This twist on grits brings to mind Frito Pie or Tex-Mex street foods. The addition of tortilla chips may shock some, but they are an important and tasty part of this recipe.

In a saucepan over medium-high heat, combine stock (or water) and a pinch of salt and bring to a boil. Slowly add cornmeal and whisk continuously for 3 minutes. Cover, reduce heat to low and cook for another 30 minutes, stirring occasionally.

Heat a grill pan over medium-high heat or preheat the barbecue to 375°F.

Meanwhile, in a medium skillet over medium-high heat, combine sausage and just enough water to cover sausage and bring to a boil. Reduce the heat to medium and cook for 10 minutes. Drain.

Place sausage in grill pan or on barbecue and cook for 8–10 minutes, turning frequently, until each side is golden.

Remove polenta from heat. Stir in butter, parsley, and Doritos. Season with salt and pepper. Transfer to a serving platter. Top with sausage and serve immediately.

VARIATION:

1 **Polenta Nachos with Braised Beef** Replace the cooked sausage with 3 cups Beer-Braised Beef Stew (page 128).

THE
BEST
DRESSED

On the farm, every season came with its own responsibilities—from sowing seeds to harvesting vegetables. We would start seedlings in old milk cartons and tie up beans with old stockings. Fresh onions and potatoes would be dug up and, with dirt under our nails, we'd lay them out in the sun to dry the skin. Once dry, we would bag the onions and potatoes in burlap to preserve them. (And without fail, the scent of burlap always triggers this memory.) While I learned a lot over those years through the harvesting of fresh vegetables at their absolute peak, I only truly valued them once I left for college.

My grandmother Evelyn Mollison had an incredible vegetable garden, and during my off-days at culinary school, I'd visit her. At the end of every afternoon together, she would send me back to the big city with a heaping bag of beets, beets, and more beets. I would prepare the simplest salads with those tender baby beets page 64 that had been picked at the beginning of the season. I was often overwhelmed by their purity and the concentration of sweetness.

Home cooks are now coming to the same realization and creating seasonally focused dishes. In this chapter, you build your culinary confidence by discovering ways of making delicious and healthy salads. Recipes such as the robust Jicama, Radish, and Kale Superfood Salad page 59 and Cauliflower and Carrot Slaw with Honey-Curry Vinaigrette page 70 are nutrient powerhouses. Roasting baby vegetables page 67 can add sweetness to a dish, while grilled watermelon page 63 pairs beautifully with Mediterranean ingredients. Build Your Own Salad Dressings page 60 will have you concocting bright, tasty vinaigrettes and dressings in no time. Eating your greens has never been this easy.

Jicama, Radish, and Kale Superfood Salad

This beautiful salad is my go-to recipe when I crave healthy food in my life. When combining salad ingredients, I often consider what the finished dish might look like—vibrant flavors paired with contrasting textures and a spectrum of color make for the most dynamic salads. Jicama—a round, bulbous root vegetable also known as the Mexican turnip—has thin brown skin and a crisp white flesh with a mild flavor between a water chestnut and an Asian pear.

To make the dressing, in a blender, combine all ingredients except oil and salt and pepper. Cover and purée until smooth. With the blender running, slowly pour in the oil and blend until emulsified. Season with salt and pepper. Pour dressing into a resealable jar and refrigerate until use. (Keeps up to 1 week in the refrigerator.)

To make the salad, in a large bowl, combine kale, radishes, carrots, jicama, fennel, peppers, corn, tomatoes, and oranges. Drizzle dressing overtop and gently toss to mix.

Sprinkle with toasted sunflower seeds (or pumpkin seeds or almonds) and serve.

Serves 4

Dressing
2 Tbsp orange juice
2 Tbsp white balsamic vinegar
1 Tbsp honey
1 tsp Dijon mustard
1 clove garlic, finely chopped
½ cup extra virgin olive oil
Salt and pepper, to taste

Salad
3 cups baby kale
½ bunch radishes, thinly sliced (1 cup)
1 carrot, cut into matchsticks (½ cup)
½ jicama, peeled and cut into matchsticks
½ head fennel, cut into matchsticks (½ cup)
½ red bell pepper, seeded and cut into matchsticks
1 corn on the cob, shucked and charred or grilled, kernels removed
½ cup cherry tomatoes, halved
1 small orange, peeled and segmented
2 Tbsp toasted sunflower seeds, pumpkin seeds, or toasted almonds, to serve

Base

Vegetable oil
Olive oil
Mayonnaise
Sour cream
Yogurt
Buttermilk
Egg yolk
Soft tofu

Salad Dressings

When making salad dressings, consider the balance of flavors: sweet, salty, sour, bitter, and umami. Think about the best ways to play ingredients off each other, and always remember: what grows together, goes together. (For instance, tomatoes and basil, strawberries and rhubarb, or peppers and eggplant.) Select one base, one acid, and mix and match different aromatics to create the ultimate customized dressings.

Serves 4

Acid

Citrus juice such as lemon, lime, or grapefruit
Fruit juice such as cranberry, pomegranate, or apple
Berries
Tomato juice
Soy sauce
Vinegar such as white, wine, balsamic, sherry, cider, rice, or champagne

Aromatics

Garlic
Shallots
Scallions
Mustards
Dry and fresh herbs
Ponzu (a citrus soy sauce, available at most supermarkets)
Yuzu sauce (spicy Japanese sauce made with yuzu and chilies, available at Asian supermarkets)
Condiments (chutneys, guacamole, ketchup, anchovy paste, wasabi paste, BBQ sauce, fish sauce)
Spices and seasonings (caraway seed, cumin, cayenne, cardamom, nutmeg, paprika, star anise, turmeric, curry powder, peppers, and salts)
Hot sauces and pastes

Summer Stack

This incredibly simple salad is always in demand. During the summer, we have the luxury of making effortless food because of the near-limitless supply of amazing fresh ingredients. The sweet and bitter lettuce pairs beautifully with the sweet raspberries and tangy Indian-flavored dressing to create a spectacular salad.

To make the vinaigrette, in a blender, combine all ingredients except oil. Cover and purée until smooth. With the blender running, slowly pour in oil and blend until emulsified. Pour dressing into a resealable jar and refrigerate until use. (Keeps up to 2 weeks in the refrigerator.)

To make the salad, on an oversized platter, stack lettuce leaves. Scatter radishes overtop. Spoon on pickled red onions. Top with avocados, mangos, and raspberries.

To make the pickled red onions, in a medium bowl, combine vinegar, sugar, and salt. Stir until sugar has dissolved. Add onions to the bowl and season with pepper. Mix well and marinate overnight at room temperature.

To serve, lightly drizzle vinaigrette overtop and garnish with cilantro.

VARIATION:

1 **Indian-Inspired Summer Stack** Add a side of grilled Tandoori Chicken (page 117) and serve with crispy poppadum (Indian chickpea crackers).

Serves 4

Chili and cilantro vinaigrette
¼ cup lime juice
½ cup sweet chili garlic sauce
1 small shallot, finely chopped
¼ cup cilantro leaves
Salt and pepper, to taste
1 cup extra virgin olive oil

Salad
2 small heads butter lettuce, washed, trimmed, and leaves separated
1 cup thinly sliced radishes
⅔ cup Pickled Red Onions
2 avocados, pitted, peeled, and diced
1 large mango, peeled and diced
1 cup raspberries
1½ cups cilantro leaves

Pickled red onions
2 cups white vinegar
¼ cup granulated sugar
Pinch of salt
4 red onions, sliced into thin rounds
Coarsely ground black pepper, to taste

Tip: For individual servings, cut the butter leaf lettuce heads in half and place each onto salad plates. Top each salad half with the assorted toppings and serve.

Grilled Watermelon
with Feta, Olives, Onion, and Basil

Serves 4

5 tsp extra virgin olive oil (divided)
1 (1-inch-thick) firm watermelon
    round, rind on
½ cup crumbled feta cheese
¼ cup pitted black olives, chopped
½ small red onion, thinly sliced
4 large basil leaves, torn
Coarsely ground black pepper,
    to taste

When we traveled to Amorgos, Greece (the easternmost of the islands), I was allowed to prepare a dish for our host's family, so I decided to make a version of this salad. They had never seen this type of salad before, but it was good enough to win over the skeptical *yia yia* (Greek for "grandmother").

This classic summer salad is elevated with the addition of grilled watermelon. Serve it warm or cold, depending on your desire and whether the salad needs to travel.

Heat a grill pan over high heat or preheat the barbecue to 400°F.

Pour 1 Tbsp olive oil into a small bowl. Lightly brush oil on one side of watermelon round. Place watermelon round on the grill, oil-side down, and grill for 1 minute. Rotate watermelon slice 45 degrees and grill for another minute. (This gives the watermelon a professional-looking crosshatched grill pattern.)

To serve, transfer watermelon to a cutting board and cut into eight wedges. Arrange on a serving platter and top with feta and olives. Scatter red onion slices and basil overtop. Season with pepper and drizzle with 2 tsp olive oil.

Enjoy like pizza wedges.

VARIATION:

1 Grilled Watermelon Salad with Feta, Bacon, Onion, and Mint
Cut small seedless watermelons into rounds to create a small salad plate. Replace the olives with crumbled bacon and replace the basil with chopped mint.

Grandma Mollison's Beet Salad

with Grapefruit and Toasted Almonds

My maternal grandmother Evelyn always served us beets, and the most impressive dish was sautéed beet tops with onions, butter, vinegar, and salt—it was both humble but crave-worthy. This recipe has been updated over the years, and I hope it becomes a cherished family recipe for you, too. It calls for tender young beet tops, which are packed with minerals and nutrients (and sweeter than the more mature plants).

To make the baby beets, in a small saucepan over medium-high heat, combine beets and salt and add enough cold water to cover. Bring to a boil. Reduce heat to medium-low and simmer for 25–30 minutes, until beets are tender and can be easily pierced with a knife. Drain and run under cold water. Remove skins and slice beets in half lengthwise.

To make the salad, place beet greens onto 4 large salad plates. Top with baby beets and grapefruit segments. In a small bowl, combine grapefruit juice, olive oil, and salt and pepper and mix well. (Alternatively, combine in a small mason jar, secure lid, and shake.)

To serve, drizzle dressing over beets and grapefruit, sprinkle with almonds, and garnish with dill. Add 2 oz smoked trout to each plate, if using, for a tasty weekend brunch dish. This recipe can also be served family style on a large, round serving platter.

Serves 4

Baby beets
1 lb baby beets, washed, trimmed, and skin on (reserve greens for the salad)
Pinch of salt

Salad
4 cups baby beet greens, washed and trimmed
2 pink grapefruit, peeled and segmented
3 Tbsp grapefruit juice
1 Tbsp extra virgin olive oil
Salt and pepper, to taste
2 Tbsp sliced skin-on almonds, toasted
2 Tbsp chopped dill
8 oz smoked trout (optional)

Tip: Replace the grapefruit segments with orange segments, or blood oranges if they are in season.

Mixed Leaf and Cucumber Salad
with Sesame and Soy Dressing

Hot days call for dishes that fill you up without weighing you down. If you want a quick-prep, high-impact salad that will impress guests, this refreshing summer salad is it. I recommend mixing and matching seasonal ingredients—the tangy Asian-inspired dressing is a perfect complement across the seasons.

To make the dressing, in a blender, combine all ingredients except vegetable oil. Cover and purée until smooth. With the blender running, slowly pour in oil and blend until emulsified. Add more sugar and sesame oil to taste. Pour dressing into a resealable jar and refrigerate until use. (Keeps up to 2 weeks in the refrigerator.)

To make the salad, shake off excess water from lettuce leaves and place in a salad spinner. Gently spin. Fan 9 cucumber rounds per plate on the outside edge of 4 salad plates. Divide lettuce leaves evenly among each plate and stack in the center, adding the smaller leaves on the top. Place carrot sticks on the top of each lettuce stack and lightly drizzle 3 Tbsp of dressing over each. Garnish with sesame seeds and chives and serve.

VARIATION:

1 Sushi Salad Chop the salad and serve over cooked sushi rice, add sashimi-grade fish and garnish with wasabi paste and pickled ginger.

Serves 4

Sesame soy dressing
½ cup rice vinegar
¼ cup soy sauce
1 Tbsp grated ginger
1 clove garlic, finely chopped
1 tsp sesame oil
1 tsp sesame seeds
1 scallion, chopped
Pinch of red pepper flakes
1 Tbsp brown sugar
2 Tbsp chopped cilantro
1 cup vegetable oil

Salad
4 large red leaf lettuce leaves, washed and trimmed
4 large green leaf lettuce leaves, washed and trimmed
4 large radicchio lettuce leaves, washed and trimmed
4 large butter lettuce leaves, washed and trimmed
4 large romaine lettuce leaves, washed and trimmed
1 small English cucumber, cut into 36 thin rounds
2 large carrots, cut into matchsticks
1 Tbsp toasted sesame seeds
1 Tbsp chopped chives

Roasted Baby Vegetables
with Burrata

Serves 4

1 lb baby carrots, scrubbed
1 lb baby beets, peeled
1 cup pearl onions
5 Tbsp extra virgin olive oil (divided)
3 Tbsp balsamic vinegar
Pinch of red pepper flakes
Salt and coarsely ground black pepper,
    to taste
6–8 oz burrata or fresh mozzarella
    cheese, whole and drained
½ cup frisée lettuce, coarsely chopped
1 Tbsp thyme leaves, torn
1 small baguette, torn into pieces

With a little sea salt, good-quality olive oil and vinegar, this dish can be served as an appetizer with just about anything. Here, the sweet baby carrots and beets, along with the chilies and vinegar, blend beautifully with the milky cheese to create a bright and vibrant salad. If there was ever a salad to share among close friends, this is it.

Preheat the oven to 400°F. Line a baking sheet with parchment paper.

To make the salad, in a large bowl, combine carrots, beets, and onions. Add 3 Tbsp olive oil, vinegar, and red pepper flakes and toss to mix. Season with salt and pepper.

Transfer to the prepared baking sheet and roast for 30–40 minutes, until tender and vegetables can be easily pierced with a knife. Set aside to cool for 5 minutes.

To serve, place burrata (or fresh mozzarella) on a cutting board, arrange roasted vegetables around the cheese and sprinkle frisée lettuce and thyme overtop. Lightly drizzle with remaining 2 Tbsp olive oil.

Enjoy with torn baguette.

VARIATION:

1 Whole Roasted Cherry Tomato and Bocconcini Salad Replace the roasted vegetables with roasted cherry tomatoes and replace the burrata with cherry bocconcini (or feta) cheese.

Vegetable Tabbouleh
with Chicken Kebab

This version of a classic tabbouleh is a great way to use up vegetables and satisfy a crowd (and kids can't always tell which vegetables are in the salad, making it a good vegetable introduction). I recommend preparing this salad a day in advance to really get the most flavor. And if chicken isn't your thing, you can replace it with fish or tofu.

To make the chicken kebab, in a large bowl, combine chicken and marinade ingredients. Skewer chicken onto four skewers. Place skewers in a resealable container or plastic bag and refrigerate for at least 3 hours or overnight.

To make the tabbouleh, in a microwave-safe bowl, combine bulgur and water. Cover with plastic wrap and microwave on high for 2–3 minutes, or until cooked through. Set aside for 5–7 minutes and then fluff with a fork. In a large bowl, combine bulgur and remaining tabbouleh ingredients. Add dressing ingredients and season with salt and pepper. Mix well and refrigerate for at least 30 minutes.

Heat a grill pan over medium-high heat or preheat the barbecue to 375°F. Lightly oil the grill pan or barbecue grates with oil (to prevent chicken from sticking). Place chicken kebab on grates. Cook for 10–12 minutes, flipping occasionally, or until cooked through and the internal temperature reaches 165°F. Season with salt and pepper.

To serve, place one round of iceberg lettuce per plate onto 4 salad plates. Top each with tabbouleh and a chicken kebab. Garnish each plate with a lemon wedge.

VARIATION:

1 Vegetable Couscous with Shrimp Kebab Replace the bulgur with couscous and the chicken with whole poached shrimp. Replace the kebab marinade with olive oil, lemon juice, and finely chopped garlic.

Serves 4

Chicken kebab
1½ lb boneless, skinless chicken
    legs, cut into 1-inch pieces
4 large metal or bamboo skewers
    (presoak bamboo skewers for
    15 minutes)
1 small head iceberg lettuce,
    cut into 4 large slices
4 large lemon wedges, to garnish

Marinade
½ cup plain yogurt
1 Tbsp extra virgin olive oil
1 tsp garlic powder
1 tsp paprika
Pinch of cayenne pepper
Pinch of ground cumin
Pinch of ground cinnamon
Pinch of ground allspice
Salt and pepper, to taste

Tabbouleh
1 cup fine bulgur wheat
2½ cups water
2 scallions, chopped
2 cloves garlic, finely chopped
1 small tomato, chopped (½ cup)
½ cup finely chopped cucumber
½ cup canned chickpeas, drained
    and rinsed
¼ cup chopped mint
1 cup chopped parsley
1 tsp cumin seeds, toasted
¼ tsp cayenne pepper

Dressing
⅔ cup olive oil
½ cup lemon juice
Salt and pepper, to taste

Cauliflower and Carrot Slaw

with Honey-Curry Vinaigrette

Serves 4

Honey-curry vinaigrette
¼ cup cider vinegar
1 clove garlic, finely chopped
2 Tbsp chopped cilantro
2 tsp curry powder
1½ tsp liquid honey
¼ tsp ground cumin
½ cup grapeseed oil
Salt and pepper, to taste

Salad
1 small head cauliflower, broken
*   into small florets*
1 cup matchstick carrots
1 cup seedless grapes, halved
½ cup golden raisins, rinsed
3 scallions, sliced

While store-bought salad kits offer convenience, the flavor of home-made salads can't be beat. This refreshing dish was inspired by afternoons wandering the exotic food shops in Toronto's Little India neighborhood.

Cauliflower is an underrated vegetable: it has a fairly neutral flavor, a good crunch, and a stability that holds up to all kinds of cooking. Here, it provides a crisp-textured base for a sweet and spicy dressing loaded with flavor.

To make the vinaigrette, in a small resealable jar, combine all dressing ingredients. Cover and shake well. (Keeps up to 2 weeks in the refrigerator.)

To make the salad, fit food processor with the slicing blade. With food processor running, feed cauliflower into the chute. (Slices should be about ⅛-inch thick.) In a large bowl, combine cauliflower, carrots, grapes, raisins, and scallions. Pour dressing over salad and toss gently to coat. Cover and refrigerate for at least 30 minutes before serving.

VARIATIONS:

1 **Shredded Slaw with Mustard and Cranberries** Replace the cauliflower with 3 cups shredded green cabbage and 2 cups thinly sliced Brussels sprouts. Replace the grapes and raisins with 1 cup dried cranberries and ½ cup sunflower seeds. In the dressing, replace the cilantro, curry powder, and cumin with 1 Tbsp grainy mustard and 4 scallions, chopped.

2 **Broccoli, Onion, and Almond Slaw** Replace the cauliflower with 1 bunch broccoli, sliced, and ½ red onion, thinly sliced. Replace the grapes and raisins with 1 cup chopped apples and ½ cup toasted sliced almonds. Add ¼ cup of mayonnaise or yogurt to the dressing. Replace the cilantro, curry powder, and cumin with ½ cup chopped parsley.

Grilled Baby Gem Lettuce
with Whipped Ricotta and Pine Nuts

How do you modernize a traditional salad and serve it at a dinner party to people with sophisticated tastes? The solution is this salad, which is an impressive upgrade of a conventional Caesar. The charred flavor of the gem lettuce pairs well with the toasted pine nuts and whipped ricotta.

To make the dressing, combine all ingredients in a small bowl and mix well. Set aside.

To make the salad, heat a grill pan over medium heat or preheat the barbecue to 375°F. Place lettuce on a large baking sheet. Season with olive oil, salt, and pepper. (Alternatively, leave raw and break into pieces, if you prefer a raw salad.)

To make the whipped ricotta, in a small bowl, combine ricotta, thyme, and lemon juice. Season with salt and pepper and stir until smooth.

To serve, place seasoned lettuce in grill pan or on barbecue, flat-side down, and grill for 2–3 minutes, or until slightly charred. Transfer lettuce to a serving platter and, working quickly, arrange tomatoes, croutons, Parmesan, and pine nuts (or black olives) on top and garnish with chopped herbs. Drizzle dressing overtop and serve warm.

Serves 4

Dressing
2 Tbsp capers, drained and chopped
2 cloves garlic, finely chopped
2 Tbsp finely grated Parmesan cheese
2 Tbsp lemon juice
1 Tbsp red wine vinegar
2 dashes Tabasco sauce
½ tsp Dijon mustard
½ cup extra virgin olive oil
Salt and pepper, to taste

Salad
4 whole heads baby gem lettuce, washed, drained, and halved
2 tsp extra virgin olive oil
Salt and pepper, to taste
1 cup cherry tomatoes, halved
¾ cup toasted croutons
¾ cup shaved Parmesan cheese
3 Tbsp toasted pine nuts or chopped black olives
½ cup chopped parsley and basil

Whipped ricotta
¼ cup ricotta cheese
¾ tsp chopped thyme
1 Tbsp lemon juice
Salt and pepper, to taste

Spinach, Prosciutto, and Sun-Dried Tomato Salad Rolls
with Black Olive Tapenade

Whether at a restaurant, a friend's house, or at home, everyone loves that this salad is served as rolls. Once you get the hang of it, it's quick to make. Not all salads have to be heavy greens and light, sweet dressings; in fact, this dark and savory dish is immensely satisfying.

To make the tapenade, in a blender, combine all ingredients except oil, olives, and pepper. Cover and purée until smooth. With the blender running, slowly pour in the oil and blend until emulsified. Add olives and pulse until olives are coarsely chopped. Season with pepper. Set aside.

To make the salad, in a medium bowl, combine spinach and sun-dried tomatoes.

On a cutting board, place 2 slices of prosciutto side-by-side to create a large sheet. Repeat with remaining slices to create a total of 4 sheets. Place 1½ cups of spinach mixture onto the short edge of each sheet. Starting at the short edge, gently roll each prosciutto sheet to form a taut roll.

To make the pepper coulis, in a blender, combine pimiento and olive oil. Cover and purée until smooth. Season with salt and pepper.

To serve, spoon equal amounts of the pepper coulis onto 4 large salad plates. Place a spinach roll on each plate and dress with 1 Tbsp tapenade. Arrange 6 cherry tomato halves beside the roll and top each roll with shaved Parmesan cheese and basil. Lightly drizzle extra virgin olive oil overtop. Pour leftover tapenade into a resealable jar and refrigerate. (Keeps up to 1 week.)

Serves 4

Black olive tapenade
1 clove garlic, chopped
1 tsp chopped shallots
¼ cup red wine vinegar
1 Tbsp Dijon mustard
Pinch of red pepper flakes
1 cup chopped parsley
¾ cup extra virgin olive oil
¾ cup Kalamata olives, pitted
Coarsely ground black pepper, to taste

Salad
6 cups baby spinach
8 sun-dried tomatoes, chopped
8 slices prosciutto
12 cherry tomatoes, halved
½ cup shaved Parmesan cheese
½ cup basil cress or basil
Extra virgin olive oil, for drizzling

Pepper coulis
¼ cup canned pimiento peppers, drained and chopped
2½ Tbsp extra virgin olive oil
Salt and pepper, to taste

COMFORT
IN A
BOWL

My home kitchen would not function without my three most-prized possessions: a cast-iron pot, my grandmother's weathered wooden spoon, and a ladle. Many of my favorite culinary storyboards have been created with those trusted utensils, and I rely on them heavily to create some of my dishes... soups.

The humblest soups have the power to satisfy our greatest cravings for comfort. These simple and nourishing one-pot meals offer the same reassurance one might find in a security blanket or worn pair of slippers. Plus, they can be elevated in extraordinary ways. Fresh aromatic herbs heighten the senses and flavor, unique ingredients such as puffed wild rice page 85 add an inventive and pleasantly surprising texture, and a slow and lazy simmer allows for the marriage of ingredients. It's no wonder I fall for these dishes time and time again.

But what I love most about them is their power to showcase seasonal produce. Spring-sown peas are deliciously sweet on their own, but will make headlines as an elegant first course in the Mint Pea Soup with Crème Fraîche and Bacon Brittle page 88. A crisp, refreshing Gazpacho with Avocado and Lime page 82 is the ultimate summer fare. Lusty, earthy mushrooms and rich, indulgent Brie may sound unconventional, but the autumnal pairing delivers a decadent and full-bodied soup page 81 that is nothing short of sublime. In winter, soups are part of my family's lifestyle, and out-of-town trips for hockey are often accompanied by thermoses of rustic, restorative Farmhouse Mason Jar Soup page 86 and bread or crackers. This is a great way to still have a family meal, even if it's in a parking lot out of town.

Tomaszeski Family Borscht

Serves 4

5 slices bacon, cut into ¼-inch cubes
½ large white onion, finely chopped
½ large carrot, cut into fine dice
3 stalks celery, cut into fine dice
1 clove garlic, finely chopped
1 lb cooked beets, shredded
2 large potatoes, cut into ¼-inch cubes
¼ small green cabbage, finely shredded
2 cups canned diced tomatoes
1 cup canned navy beans, drained and
    rinsed
6 cups beef stock
Salt and pepper, to taste
4 oz leftover roast beef, cut into ½-inch
    cubes (1 cup)
White vinegar, to taste
¼ cup finely chopped dill
½ cup chopped scallions
½ cup sour cream
Warm bread, to serve

By far, my most requested recipe is one that I didn't even invent: a classic borscht I used to have when visiting my baba. The original recipe was from a very old cookbook, but Baba's version (which I've spent a lifetime trying to recreate) tasted out of this world. The smell of beets always brings me back to those meals spent with her.

In a large saucepan over medium-high heat, cook bacon for 5–7 minutes, until crispy. Add onions, carrots, celery, and garlic and cook for another 5 minutes. Add beets, potatoes, cabbage, tomatoes, beans, and beef stock and bring to a boil.

Season lightly with salt and pepper. Add roast beef, reduce heat to medium-low and simmer, uncovered, for 1 hour.

Remove the soup from the heat. Season with more salt and pepper, if desired, and vinegar. Ladle into 4 bowls and garnish with dill, scallions, and sour cream. Serve with warm bread.

VARIATION:

1 Cold Borscht with Egg and Cream Serve the soup cold with chopped dill and boiled egg, and replace the sour cream with a splash of cream.

Black Bean and Lentil Soup

with Smashed Avocado and Corn Tortillas

Serves 4

1 Tbsp olive oil
½ small white onion, chopped
½ small carrot, cut into ½-inch dice
1 stalk celery, cut into ½-inch dice
1 clove garlic, finely chopped
Salt and pepper, to taste
½ tsp ground paprika
1 tsp ground cumin
Cayenne pepper, to taste
Red pepper flakes, to taste
1¾ cups canned diced tomatoes
1 (19-oz) can black beans or any type of
    bean, drained and rinsed
¼ cup dried lentils
4 cups vegetable stock
2 Tbsp finely chopped cilantro
1 ripened avocado, pitted and peeled
1 cup blue corn tortilla chips, crumbled
Pulled BBQ pork or chicken, to serve
    (optional)

Modern-day Mexican food is rooted in Indigenous and European ingredients. This recipe is a tribute to the traditional flavors we have grown to love. Best served on cold winter nights, this nourishing and warming soup comes to life with spices, heat, and vibrant cilantro.

In a large saucepan over medium-high heat, heat oil. Add onions, carrots, and celery and sauté for 5 minutes, until onions are softened and translucent. Add garlic and cook for 2–3 minutes, until fragrant. Season with salt and pepper. Stir in paprika, cumin, cayenne, and red pepper flakes and cook for 3–5 minutes, until onions have started to brown and spices are fragrant.

Add tomatoes, black beans (or other type of beans), lentils, and vegetable stock and bring to a boil. Reduce heat to medium-low and simmer for 30–40 minutes.

Remove soup from the heat. Using a hand blender, carefully blitz soup until smooth. (Alternatively, leave it as is for a chunky soup.) Season with more salt and pepper, if desired, then stir in cilantro.

Scoop avocado into a small bowl, smash with a fork, and set aside. Ladle soup into 4 bowls. Garnish with tortilla chips and avocado and serve hot with pulled BBQ pork or chicken, if using.

VARIATIONS:

1 Black Bean, Lentil, and Beef Soup with Cheddar and Corn Tortillas Add ½ lb ground beef to the onion mixture and cook thoroughly. Replace the avocado with 1 cup grated cheddar cheese.

2 Black Bean and Lentil Soup with Sour Cream, Scallions, and Corn Tortillas Eliminate the avocado and serve the soup with a dollop of sour cream and chopped scallions.

Chicken and Dumpling Soup

My mother is second to none at making dumplings. Hers are billowy clouds that float to the surface of the soup, and as a kid I used to ration out the bites of dumplings. This cheap and cheerful soup tastes like it's made with love.

Southern American cooking doesn't necessarily involve expensive produce or tons of spices—it's about applying techniques that coax out flavor from the humblest of ingredients.

To make the soup, in a large saucepan over medium-high heat, heat butter and oil. Sauté onions for 5 minutes, until softened and translucent. Add carrots, celery, and garlic and cook for another minute.

Add peppers, potatoes, and mushrooms and cook for another 3–5 minutes, until peppers are softened and mushrooms are reduced. Add chicken stock and cooked chicken and bring to a boil. Reduce heat to medium-low and simmer for 40 minutes, uncovered, until vegetables are almost cooked through.

To make the dumplings, in a medium bowl, combine dumpling ingredients. Mix until a soft dough forms. Carefully drop heaping spoonfuls of dough into soup. Reduce heat to low. Cover and simmer for 15 minutes, until dumplings double in size. Stir in cilantro.

Remove soup from the heat. Season with salt and pepper and serve immediately.

VARIATION:

1 **Chicken Soup with Israeli Couscous** Replace the dumplings with 1 cup Israeli couscous.

Serves 4

Soup
1½ Tbsp butter (divided)
1 Tbsp extra virgin olive oil
½ small white onion, finely chopped
½ large carrot, finely chopped
1 stalk celery, finely chopped
1 clove garlic, finely chopped
2 red bell peppers, seeded and finely chopped
1 large Yukon Gold potato, finely chopped
½ cup assorted mushrooms such as shiitake and field, thinly sliced
6 cups chicken stock
¾ cup cooked chicken, white and dark meat shredded (or any roasted meat)
¼ bunch cilantro, finely chopped
Salt and pepper, to taste

Dumplings
½ cup all-purpose flour
½ tsp baking powder
3 Tbsp milk
½ Tbsp finely chopped parsley
Salt and pepper, to taste

Creamy Mushroom Bisque

with Torched Brie

The marriage of cream with the umami of mushrooms is irresistible, so it comes as no surprise that this mushroom bisque has universal appeal. The torched Brie takes this from a weekday dinner to a special occasion meal, so I tend to make it when we have guests. This recipe was my reinvention of French onion soup: the traditional Gruyère toasts and caramelized onions are replaced with torched Brie and mushrooms. Not only is it faster to make, it has a more luxurious quality to it.

In a large saucepan over medium-high heat, heat oil and butter. Add onions and leeks, and sauté for 5 minutes, until onions are softened and translucent. Add mushrooms and sauté for another 5 minutes.

Stir in flour, then pour in stock and wine. Using a balloon whisk, whisk until smooth.

Add potatoes and simmer, uncovered, for 30–40 minutes, until potatoes are tender and soup is slightly thickened. (Stir occasionally to prevent soup from scorching or sticking to the bottom of the saucepan.)

Meanwhile, preheat broiler to high heat.

Remove soup from the heat. Stir in cream and Parmesan. Season with salt and pepper.

Ladle soup into 4 heatproof bowls. Top each bowl with a slice of bread and a slice of Brie. Place the bowls under broiler for 1 minute, or until the cheese melts. Serve immediately.

VARIATIONS:

1 Creamy Cauliflower (or Broccoli) Bisque with Torched Brie
Replace the mushrooms with an equal amount of cauliflower or broccoli florets.

2 French Onion Soup Eliminate the mushrooms, add 2 large onions, and replace Brie with equal amounts of grated Swiss, Emmental, or Gruyère cheese.

Serves 4

1 Tbsp extra virgin olive oil
1 Tbsp butter
½ small white onion, finely chopped
½ leek, thinly sliced
1 cup cremini mushrooms, thinly sliced
½ cup shiitake mushrooms, thinly sliced
½ cup oyster mushrooms, chopped
½ cup portobello mushrooms, chopped
¼ cup chanterelle mushrooms, chopped (optional)
1½ Tbsp all-purpose flour
3 cups vegetable or chicken stock
1 cup dry white wine
5 small Yukon Gold potatoes, peeled and diced
½ cup whipping (35%) cream
½ cup Parmesan cheese, finely grated
Salt and pepper, to taste
4 (½-inch-thick) slices sourdough bread, toasted
2 oz Brie cheese, sliced into 4 equal pieces

Gazpacho
with Avocado and Lime

Gazpacho is a refreshingly vibrant chilled soup that makes the most of summer's bountiful tomatoes, cucumbers, and peppers—especially on days when you're pressed for time and looking for ingredients to come together in a flash. This Tex-Mex version is enhanced with the addition of avocado and lime.

In a food processor, combine tomatoes, tomato juice, garlic, lime juice, oil, hot sauce, and cilantro. Process until smooth. Season with salt and pepper. Pour into a large bowl, stir in onions, cucumbers, and red peppers. Season with more salt and pepper, if desired, then chill for at least 30 minutes in the refrigerator.

Ladle soup into 4 glass tumblers. Top with avocado and chopped cilantro and serve. (Alternatively, serve gazpacho in shot glasses to create a unique between-meal palate cleanser at dinner parties.)

VARIATION:

1 Watermelon and Feta Gazpacho Replace plum tomatoes with equal amounts of puréed watermelon and garnish each bowl with crumbled feta cheese.

Serves 4

4 ripe plum tomatoes, stemmed and cored
2 cups tomato juice
1 clove garlic
3 Tbsp lime juice
1 Tbsp extra virgin olive oil
1 tsp hot sauce
½ cup finely chopped cilantro, plus extra to garnish
½ small red onion, finely chopped
Salt and pepper, to taste
1 English cucumber, peeled, seeded, and finely chopped
1 red bell pepper, seeded and finely chopped
½ avocado, pitted, peeled, and cut into ¼-inch cubes

Potato and Corn Chowder

with Smoked Paprika and Puffed Wild Rice

Serves 4

2 Tbsp olive oil
½ small white onion, finely chopped
6 slices smoked bacon, chopped,
   or 1 cup chopped ham (optional)
1 clove garlic, finely chopped
½ small leek, finely chopped
1 tsp smoked paprika
3 stalks celery, finely chopped
½ cup Yukon Gold potatoes, chopped
1 small sweet potato, peeled and
   chopped
1½ cups fresh or frozen sweet corn
1 small carrot, chopped
½ small parsnip, chopped
½ cup butternut squash, peeled,
   seeded, and chopped
8 cups vegetable stock
½ cup whipping (35%) cream (optional)
Salt and pepper, to taste
2 Tbsp finely chopped parsley
2 Tbsp finely chopped chives
1 Tbsp vegetable oil
¼ cup wild rice

This easy soup is an inventive way to savor the bounty of summer—
and a nod to my childhood, when late summer was often spent picking
corn from the fields. The sweet potatoes and smoked paprika make the
taste of this theatrical soup as surprising as the texture of the puffed
wild rice garnish. (Wild rice explodes when applied to direct heat,
much like popcorn.)

In a large saucepan over medium-high heat, heat oil. Add onions and
bacon (or ham), if using, and sauté for 3–5 minutes, until onions are
softened and translucent. Add garlic, leeks, and smoked paprika and
sauté for 3–4 minutes, until leeks are softened.

Add celery, potatoes, corn, carrots, parsnips, and squash. Pour in
stock and cream, if using, and bring to a boil. Reduce heat to low and
simmer for 30–40 minutes, until vegetables are tender. Remove soup
from the heat. Season with salt and pepper and stir in parsley and chives.

In a medium skillet over medium-high heat, heat oil. Add wild rice,
cover, and shake vigorously to thoroughly coat the rice. Shake for
2–3 minutes, until the wild rice pops. Remove from the heat and set aside.

Ladle soup into 4 bowls, top each with puffed wild rice and serve.

VARIATION:

1 Curried Ham and Potato Chowder with Puffed Wild Rice
Add ¾ cup smoked ham and replace the smoked paprika with
curry powder or ground cumin.

Farmhouse Mason Jar Soup

When you live a hectic lifestyle, it always helps to have a stocked pantry. As a chef, sometimes the last thing I want to do when I return home is devise a recipe for dinner. This soup is a perfect solution for those occasions.

Prep the jars of soup in advance so they come in handy for last-minute meals at home or at the cottage—simply replace the canned beans and chickpeas with ½ cup dried.

In a large saucepan over medium-high heat, heat oil. Add onions and sauté for 4–5 minutes, until softened and translucent. Add carrots, celery, and garlic and sauté for 4–5 minutes, until celery is softened.

Add the bay leaves, dehydrated onion, basil, parsley, oregano, thyme, kidney beans, chickpeas, orzo, rice, sun-dried tomatoes, crushed tomatoes, and stock and bring to a boil. Reduce heat to low and simmer for 15–30 minutes, until vegetables, pasta, and rice are cooked. Season with salt and pepper.

Stir in parsley, then ladle soup into 4 bowls. Sprinkle with Parmesan cheese and serve.

VARIATION:

1. **Tex-Mex Soup** Replace the dried herbs with an equal amount of taco seasoning.

Serves 4

2 Tbsp extra virgin olive oil
1 small white onion, finely chopped
1 large carrot, chopped
1 stalk celery, chopped
3 cloves garlic, finely chopped
2 bay leaves
2 Tbsp dehydrated onion
2 Tbsp thinly sliced basil (or 2 tsp dried)
2 Tbsp finely chopped parsley (or 1 tsp dried)
1 Tbsp finely chopped oregano (or 1 tsp dried)
1 Tbsp finely chopped thyme leaves (or 1 tsp dried)
1 can red kidney beans, drained and rinsed (or ½ cup dried)
1 can chickpeas, drained and rinsed (or ½ cup dried)
½ cup orzo pasta
½ cup long-grain white rice
½ cup sun-dried tomatoes, coarsely chopped
1 (28-oz) can crushed tomatoes
6 cups vegetable stock
Salt and pepper, to taste
2 Tbsp finely chopped parsley
¼ cup shaved Parmesan cheese

Tip: Measure and place all dried ingredients, except for orzo and rice, in a large mason jar and store. When ready to use, prepare fresh ingredients according to recipe. Add contents of the mason jar, sun-dried tomatoes, crushed tomatoes, and vegetable stock. Bring soup to a boil, reduce heat to low and simmer for 30 minutes. Add orzo and rice and simmer for 30 minutes, until beans and chickpeas are tender. Season to taste with salt and pepper.

Roasted Red Pepper and Sweet Potato Soup
with Grilled Halloumi

Serves 4

1 small white onion, coarsely
    chopped
2 red bell peppers, seeded and
    coarsely chopped
2 small sweet potatoes, peeled
    and coarsely chopped
2 cloves garlic, peeled
2 Tbsp extra virgin olive oil
Salt and pepper, to taste
2 oz halloumi cheese, cut into
    ¼-inch slices
6 cups hot vegetable stock
2 Tbsp finely chopped parsley

Entertaining can be daunting if you don't feel confident in the kitchen. This magical recipe requires very little skill, but will have your guests talking about it well after your dinner party. Halloumi is a savory, semi-hard cheese that's robust enough to withstand high-heat cooking and still retain its shape—it also happens to be delicious and extremely easy to prepare.

Heat a grill pan over medium-high heat or preheat the barbecue to 375°F. Preheat the oven to 425°F. Line a baking sheet with parchment paper.

In a large bowl, combine onions, peppers, potatoes, and garlic. Drizzle oil overtop and season with salt and pepper. Toss to mix. Spread vegetables on the prepared baking sheet. Roast for 45 minutes, or until the vegetables are tender and golden brown around the edges.

Place halloumi in grill pan or on barbecue and grill for 2 minutes. Flip and grill for another minute. Remove from heat and set aside.

Transfer roasted vegetables to a food processor. Pour hot stock into food processor and process until smooth. Using a fine-mesh sieve, strain soup into a large pot. Bring to a boil over medium-high heat. Reduce heat to low and simmer for 10 minutes. Season with salt and pepper, to taste.

Ladle soup into 4 bowls. Top each with a piece of grilled halloumi, garnish with chopped parsley and serve.

VARIATION:

1 Roasted Red Pepper and Potato Soup with Goat Cheese Eliminate the halloumi cheese and replace the sweet potatoes with an equal amount of yellow potatoes. Replace the parsley with 1 Tbsp of fresh thyme or ½ Tbsp dried sumac and garnish with crumbled goat cheese.

Mint Pea Soup
with Crème Fraîche and Bacon Brittle

Peas are one of the best things about summer, but this light and delicious soup is perfect no matter the time of year. The addition of crème fraîche and bacon brittle makes this soup even more luxurious and perfect for entertaining. If you are serving this to company, make everything ahead of time and then simply heat, garnish, and serve.

To make the crème fraîche, in a mason jar, combine cream and buttermilk and stir. Cover and set aside at room temperature (approximately 70°F) for 8–24 hours, or until the mixture is very thick. (I recommend preparing it the night before.)

To make the soup, in a large saucepan over medium-high heat, heat butter and oil. Add leeks and shallots and sauté for 3–4 minutes, until tender. Add potatoes and sauté for 2–3 minutes.

Pour in stock and bring to a boil. Reduce heat to medium-low and simmer for 20–25 minutes, until potatoes are tender. Stir in peas, spinach, and mint. Cook for 15 minutes.

Meanwhile, make the bacon brittle. Preheat the oven to 325°F. Line a baking sheet with parchment paper.

In a small bowl, combine bacon, brown sugar, and pepper and stir until bacon is coated. Lay bacon strips on the prepared baking sheet, making sure they are flat. Place a piece of parchment paper on top of the bacon. Place another baking sheet on top of the parchment paper so that the two baking sheets are nestled together. (This keeps the bacon flat while cooking.) Bake for 20–30 minutes, until bacon is browned and crispy. (Check every 10–15 minutes to prevent overcooking.) Remove from oven. Remove top baking sheet and allow bacon to cool. Crumble the bacon brittle and set aside.

Working in batches, transfer the soup to a blender and purée until smooth. Using a fine-mesh sieve, strain soup back into saucepan. Season with salt and pepper. Stir in lemon juice.

Ladle into 4 bowls. Garnish with a dollop of crème fraîche and bacon brittle, and drizzle olive oil on top (if using). Soup can be served warm or cold.

VARIATION:

1 Chilled Mint Pea Soup with Sour Cream and Bacon Brittle
Replace the crème fraîche with sour cream and serve chilled.

Serves 4

Crème fraîche
1 cup whipping (35%) cream
2 Tbsp buttermilk

Soup
1 Tbsp butter
1 Tbsp extra virgin olive oil
1 small leek, sliced
1 shallot, finely chopped
1 large Yukon Gold potato, cut into
  ½ inch cubes
4 cups vegetable stock
1½ cups frozen peas
1 cup spinach
¼ cup finely chopped mint
Juice of ½ lemon
Extra virgin olive oil, to garnish
  (optional)

Bacon brittle
4 thick slices bacon
1 Tbsp brown sugar
Pepper, to taste

Stone Soup Three Ways

The story of stone soup is one of a community pulling together ingredients to make a delicious soup that everyone can share, and these recipes will show you how to extend your roasts in delicious ways.

Some of the best dishes can be made economically, and nothing is more cost-effective than scraps and leftovers from a meal the night before. Conqee is an Asian rice-based porridge that can be made with water or stock and soaks up the flavor of anything you add to it. The beef and barley soup is ideal when you have leftover beef from prime rib, steaks, or a roast. Split pea and ham is a great example of how to use leftover ingredients to make an outstanding dish.

Serves 4

Turkey Congee

1 turkey carcass, broken into large pieces
1 cup long-grain white rice
8 cups cold water
6 thin slices ginger (divided)
6 scallions, sliced lengthwise (divided)
Salt, to taste
1 Tbsp sesame oil

Preheat the oven to 400°F.

Put carcass in a roasting pan and roast, uncovered, for 25–30 minutes, until bones are golden brown. Remove and set aside.

In a large saucepan over medium-high heat, combine carcass, rice, water, 4 ginger slices and 4 scallion slices and bring to a boil. Reduce heat to low and simmer, uncovered, for 1 hour, stirring occasionally, until thick and creamy. Remove carcass and season with salt. Cut the remaining 2 ginger slices into matchsticks and chop the scallions.

Ladle congee into 4 bowls. Top with ginger and scallions. Drizzle with sesame oil and serve.

Beef Barley Soup

Stock
2 Tbsp extra virgin olive oil
1 rack prime rib bones, cut into pieces
1 white onion, coarsely chopped
1 carrot, coarsely chopped
1 stalk celery, coarsely chopped
1 clove garlic, crushed
8 cups cold water
2 sprigs thyme
1 bay leaf
¼ bunch parsley stems
¼ tsp black peppercorns

Soup
1 Tbsp extra virgin olive oil
1 lb leftover prime rib, cut into ½-inch cubes
1 large carrot, finely chopped
3 stalks celery, finely chopped
1 large white onion, finely chopped
2 cloves garlic, finely chopped
½ cup pearl barley
Salt and pepper, to taste
2 Tbsp finely chopped parsley

Preheat the oven to 425°F.

To make the stock, in a roasting pan, combine oil, bones, onions, carrots, celery, and garlic. Roast for 25–30 minutes, until bones and vegetables are golden brown. (Stir occasionally to prevent burning.) Remove and set aside.

In a large saucepan over medium-high heat, combine roasted bones and vegetables, water, thyme, bay leaf, parsley stems, and peppercorns and bring to a boil. Reduce heat to low and simmer, uncovered, for 4 hours, skimming foam and fat from the surface as needed. Using a fine-mesh sieve, strain soup back into saucepan and set aside.

To make the soup, in a large saucepan over medium-high heat, heat oil. Add prime rib and sauté for 3 minutes, until browned. Add carrots, celery, onions, and garlic and sauté for 2–3 minutes, until the vegetables are slightly browned. Add the beef stock and pearl barley and bring to a boil. Reduce the heat to low and simmer for 30 minutes, until barley and vegetables are tender. Season with salt and pepper.

Garnish with parsley and serve.

Split Pea and Ham Soup

1 lb leftover ham bone with some meat
1 Tbsp extra virgin olive oil
1 small white onion, finely chopped
1 carrot, finely chopped
2 stalks celery, finely chopped
1 clove garlic, finely chopped
2 cups dried split peas
1 bay leaf
6 cups cold water
1 cup baby spinach
Salt and pepper, to taste
2 Tbsp finely chopped parsley or 2 scallions, finely sliced

Preheat the oven to 425°F.

Put bone in a roasting pan and roast for 25–30 minutes, until bone is golden brown. Remove and set aside.

In a large saucepan over medium-high heat, heat oil. Add onions, carrots, celery, and garlic, and sauté for 3–5 minutes, until onions are softened and translucent. Add bone, peas, bay leaf, and water and bring to a boil. Reduce heat to low and simmer, uncovered, for 1½ hours, until peas break down and meat falls off the bone.

Remove bone from soup. Pull off any remaining meat and cut into small pieces. Set aside.

Working in batches, transfer soup to a blender, add spinach, and purée until smooth. Return blended soup to the saucepan and add ham. Season with salt and pepper.

Ladle soup into 4 bowls. Garnish with parsley (or scallions) and serve.

THE
LUNCH
HOUR

Lunch service at Holt Renfrew and the hotels I've worked in was the most frenzied time of my day for many years. Our kitchen would transform into a war room during those hours as dish after dish was executed and churned out to exacting standards. And because the clientele had an insatiable desire for the new and the unusual, some of my strangest and most innovative dishes originated from those experiences.

Tartines page 98 brought sanity to our kitchen. These easy-to-assemble, open-faced sandwiches come in endless variations to satiate our patrons just enough for the remainder of the afternoon (which was often spent trying on clothes). At the Westin Harbour Castle Hotel, our Tiffin Tins page 107 appealed to those guests who required take-out lunches.

Most people invest the shortest amount of time and effort into lunch. It's the quickest meal of the day, and the second heaviest, and is often eaten at a desk or on the road (if you have kids in basketball, this is a large part of your life), but injecting a little fun into it only requires a bit more effort. The seafood-laden Bouillabaisse page 97 flavors will take you to the coast; a CT Burger with Onion Jam page 102 will stay with you right through the afternoon; and an exciting Farro Bowl with Chickpeas, Carrots, Crème Fraîche, Mint, and Basil page 94 will bring any meal to life.

Farro Bowl
with Chickpeas, Carrots, Crème Fraîche, Mint, and Basil

Alberta is a place where thousands of miles of land are covered by grains, and I've always enjoyed working with them. And inspiration for many of my dishes comes from my travels. Whenever I visit Vancouver, I like to discover new, trendy dishes, and power bowls seem to be everywhere. The idea is simple: a bed of grains topped with energy-giving vegetables and an addictive dressing. I recommend preparing the crème fraîche the night before.

To make the crème fraîche, in a glass container, combine cream and buttermilk and stir well. Cover and allow to stand at room temperature (approximately 70°F) for 8–24 hours, until thickened.

To make the farro bowl, preheat the oven to 400°F. Line a baking sheet with parchment paper.

Spread the carrots onto the prepared baking sheet. Drizzle oil overtop and season with salt and pepper. Roast for 15–20 minutes, until tender.

In a medium saucepan over high heat, combine farro and chicken stock (or water) and bring to a boil. Reduce to low heat and simmer for 20 minutes, until tender. Drain and set aside to cool.

To make the vinaigrette, put lemon juice in a small bowl and whisk in oil. Add lemon zest and season with salt and pepper.

To serve, in a large bowl, combine farro, carrots, spinach, chickpeas, basil, and mint. Toss to mix. Divide among 4 bowls, lightly drizzle vinaigrette overtop, and top with a dollop of crème fraîche.

VARIATION:

1 **Bean Medley or Barley Power Bowl** Replace the farro with 1 cup mixed beans or cooked barley.

Serves 4

Crème fraîche
1 cup whipping (35%) cream
2 Tbsp buttermilk

Farro bowl
2 carrots, cut into ¼-inch rounds
1 Tbsp olive oil
Salt and pepper, to taste
1 cup farro, rinsed
3 cups chicken stock or water
4 cups fresh spinach, washed and dried
2 cups canned chickpeas, drained and rinsed
1 cup torn basil leaves
1 cup torn mint leaves

Lemon vinaigrette
1 lemon, zested and juiced
2 Tbsp extra virgin olive oil
Salt and pepper, to taste

Maple-Glazed Salmon
with Cucumber and Ponzu Salad

Ponzu—a Japanese citrus sauce that packs a flavorful punch—can be purchased at Asian grocery stores or the Asian food aisle of larger grocery stores. The Japanese are world-renowned for their fish recipes, and this recipe applies a classic flavor profile to a very Canadian ingredient. Rich in omega-3 fatty acids, salmon is perfectly suited for a light and tasty dinner.

To make the salmon, in a shallow baking dish, combine all ingredients, except salmon and oil. Mix well. Add salmon and coat on all sides. Cover baking dish with plastic wrap and marinate in the refrigerator for 4–6 hours.

To make the dressing, in a medium bowl, combine all ingredients. Whisk until the sugar is dissolved. Add cucumbers, onions, and chives. Gently toss to mix. Set aside.

Heat a grill pan over medium-high heat or preheat the barbecue to 375°F

Remove salmon from the baking dish, shaking off excess marinade.

Lightly oil the grill pan or barbecue grates. Place fillets in grill pan or on barbecue and cook for 5 minutes. Flip and cook for another 5–6 minutes, until cooked through (fish will be firm and flake easily).

Place one salmon fillet per plate onto 4 plates. Serve with cucumber salad.

VARIATION:

1 Maple-Glazed Shrimp with Cucumber and Ponzu Salad
Replace the salmon with peeled shrimp.

Serves 4

Salmon
1 orange, zested and juiced
2 Tbsp pure maple syrup
2 Tbsp light soy sauce
2 small cloves garlic, finely chopped
1 tsp grated ginger
Pinch of red pepper flakes
2 Tbsp chopped cilantro
Salt and pepper, to taste
4 (5-oz) skinless salmon fillets
2 Tbsp canola oil

Dressing
2 Tbsp ponzu
2 Tbsp rice vinegar
1 tsp sugar
2 Tbsp sesame seeds
½ tsp sesame oil
Pinch of salt

Cucumber and ponzu salad
2 baby cucumbers, peeled, halved, and sliced
½ small red onion, thinly sliced
2 Tbsp chopped chives

Bouillabaisse

The origin of bouillabaisse is a classic tale of ingenuity: fishermen would come back with their catch and prepare a quick soup with some sea water, vegetables, and spices. The anise-flavoring of the Pernod combined with the warmth of saffron add depth to this rich and zingy summertime dish.

In a small bowl, combine saffron and hot water. Set aside to infuse.

In a large saucepan over medium-high heat, heat oil. Add onions, carrots, and celery and sauté for 5 minutes, until onions are softened and translucent. Add fennel bulb, garlic, bay leaf, and red and green bell peppers and sauté for 2–3 minutes.

Pour in Clamato (or tomato juice), tomatoes, vegetable stock, wine, Pernod, and saffron mixture and bring to a boil. Reduce heat to medium-low and simmer, uncovered, for 30–40 minutes.

Add fish and seafood. Cover and cook for 3–4 minutes, or until seafood is cooked and mussels and clams have opened. (Discard any mussels and clams that have not opened.) Season with salt and pepper.

Ladle soup into 4 oversized bowls, evenly distributing fish and seafood. Garnish with finely chopped fennel fronds and serve immediately with crusty bread.

VARIATION:

1 **Fisherman's Stew** Add 2 baby potatoes, halved, to the soup with the carrots and celery and garnish with basil and fennel fronds.

Serves 4

Pinch of saffron
1 Tbsp hot water
¼ cup extra virgin olive oil
½ large white onion, finely chopped
1 large carrot, cut into small dice
4 stalks celery, cut into small dice
½ bulb of fennel, roughly chopped, fronds reserved to garnish
2 cloves garlic, finely chopped
1 bay leaf
½ red bell pepper, seeded and cut into ¼-inch cubes
½ green bell pepper, seeded and cut into ¼-inch cubes
4 cups Clamato or tomato juice
4 cups canned diced tomatoes
4 cups vegetable stock
½ cup dry white wine
½ cup Pernod
6 oz red snapper fillet, cut into 2-inch pieces
6 oz white fish fillet (such as cod or halibut), cut into 2-inch pieces
20 mussels, scrubbed and debearded
16 (size 2½) tail-on shrimp, peeled and deveined
16 littleneck clams, cleaned
12 scallops
Salt and pepper, to taste
Crusty bread, to serve

Four Season Tartines

More than any other dish, the tartine has defined my career. At my first work experience in France, I was assigned to making these simple yet attractive open-faced sandwiches, and I didn't speak a word of French. I quickly learned the value of high-quality ingredients, the importance of detail, and the essentials of efficiency within a limited space.

While working at Holt Renfrew, I had customers who'd come to the restaurant three or four times a week. I added tartines to the menu because they were quick to prepare and versatile enough to switch up the flavors regularly so frequent customers never got bored. They were also made with famed Poilâne bread, which was couriered to us from Paris every two days.

These variations are a celebration of the seasons. For the chicken and truffle-honey tartine, spring's produce is anchored by chèvre (soft goat cheese) and a light protein; while the warm Caprese variation makes the most of summer's bountiful tomatoes. Fall brings us earthy flavors to be enjoyed on a crisp, clear day, and mushrooms team with feta and caramelized onions for an arguably more rustic tartine. And lastly, smoked salmon always reminds me of the holidays and this winter version is an ode to memories of family gatherings. (See image on page 101.)

Serves 4

1

SPRING

Chicken and Truffle-Honey Tartine

4 (¼-inch-thick) slices sourdough bread
6 Tbsp chèvre (soft goat cheese)
4 (3–4-oz) cooked chicken breasts, thinly sliced
4 cups arugula leaves
2 large red bell peppers, seeded and cut into thin strips
¼ cup Truffle Honey (page 196)

To toast bread, preheat broiler to high heat. Place bread on a baking sheet and toast for 2–3 minutes, until golden.

Spread 1½ Tbsp of chèvre onto each slice of toasted bread. Top with sliced chicken breast, arugula, and red pepper strips.

Lightly drizzle truffle honey over each tartine. Carefully cut tartines into quarters and serve warm.

2

SUMMER

Warm Caprese Tartine

4 (¼-inch thick) slices sourdough bread
6 Tbsp Aioli (page 196)
12 oz bocconcini or buffalo mozzarella,
  sliced into 12 slices
12 Roasted Plum Tomatoes (page 197)
Salt, to taste
½ cup basil leaves, torn

To toast bread, preheat broiler to high heat. Put the bread on a baking sheet and toast for 2–3 minutes, until golden.

Spread 1½ Tbsp of aioli onto each slice of toasted bread. Top each with bocconcini (or mozzarella) and roasted tomatoes. Toast in the oven for 2 minutes, until the cheese begins to melt and the tomatoes are warmed.

To finish, season with salt and sprinkle basil overtop. Cut tartines into quarters and serve warm.

3

FALL

Mushroom, Caramelized Onion, and Feta Tartine

4 (¼-inch thick) slices sourdough bread
1 cup Caramelized Onions (page 196)
2 cups Sautéed Mushrooms (page 197)
6 Tbsp crumbled feta
2 cups chopped frisée lettuce
1 cup Crispy Leeks (page 196)

To toast bread, preheat broiler to high heat. Place bread on a baking sheet and toast for 2–3 minutes, until golden.

Spread ¼ cup of caramelized onions onto each slice of toasted bread. Top with sautéed mushrooms, feta, and frisée.

Sprinkle crispy leeks overtop. Cut tartines into quarters and serve warm.

4

WINTER

Smoked Salmon, Brussels Sprouts, and Poached Egg Tartine

4 (¼-inch thick) slices sourdough bread
4 tsp butter
8 oz smoked salmon, sliced
8 Poached Eggs (page 36)
1 cup Sautéed Brussels Sprouts
  (page 196)
1 cup fresh chopped herbs

To toast bread, preheat broiler to high heat. Place bread on a baking sheet and toast for 2–3 minutes, until golden.

Spread 1 tsp of butter onto each slice of toasted bread. Top each with salmon and 2 poached eggs.

Spoon sautéed Brussels sprouts over each tartine and garnish with chopped herbs. Cut each tartine in half and serve.

CT Burger
with Onion Jam

Serves 4

Onion jam
1 Tbsp butter
2 large onions, chopped
1 tsp granulated sugar
2 Tbsp red wine vinegar
Salt and pepper, to taste

Garlic mayonnaise
1 head Roasted Garlic (page 196)
2 cups mayonnaise

Patties
1½ lb extra-lean ground chuck beef
2 shallots, finely chopped
1 clove garlic, finely chopped
2 Tbsp cold butter, cut into ¼-inch
  cubes
2 Tbsp finely chopped rosemary
1 Tbsp finely chopped thyme
Salt and pepper, to taste

To serve
4 (½-oz) slices cheddar cheese
4 large brioche-style buns
4 large leaves green leaf lettuce
1 tomato, cut into ⅛-inch slices
4 dill pickles

This recipe for my eponymous burger was put on the menu at C5 restaurant at the Royal Ontario Museum in Toronto. If you want to make your burger upscale, look for ways to coax flavor from your cut. Here, extra-lean ground chuck is cut with chilled butter so the burger self-bastes during the cooking process. The result? A moist and flavorful burger that's practically foolproof and quickly put together for an easy weekday meal (or party dish). The onion jam adds a perfect amount of sweetness.

To make the onion jam, in a skillet over medium heat, melt butter. Add onions and sauté for 10–12 minutes, until softened and caramelized. Add sugar and vinegar and season with salt and pepper. Cook for another 2 minutes. Remove from heat and set aside to cool. (Jam keeps up to 2 weeks in the refrigerator.)

To make the garlic mayonnaise, using your thumb and index finger, squeeze out garlic cloves into a medium bowl. Add mayonnaise and mash.

To make the patties, in a medium bowl, combine all ingredients and mix well. Form 4 equal-sized patties, about 1-inch thick. Heat a grill pan over medium-high heat or preheat the barbecue to 375°F. Place patties in grill pan or on barbecue and cook for 4 minutes. Flip and cook for another 4 minutes, until nearly cooked through. Top each patty with a slice of cheese and cook for another minute, until cheese is melted.

Meanwhile, toast the buns on the hot grill.

To serve, brush the bottom half of each bun with 1 tsp garlic mayonnaise. Line with lettuce and sliced tomatoes and top with the patties. Spoon 1 Tbsp of onion jam on each patty and top with the other half of the buns. Serve with dill pickles.

VARIATIONS:

1 **Lamb Burger with Feta** Replace the ground beef with ground lamb and add ½ cup crumbled feta cheese to the patty mixture.

2 **CT Burger with Lemon Mayo, Pesto, and Grilled Onions and Peppers** Eliminate the onion jam, replace the garlic mayonnaise with lemon mayonnaise (page 118), and brush 1 tsp of basil pesto on each bun. Top with grilled onions and peppers.

Rotisserie Chicken Three Ways

Inexpensive and reliable ready-made rotisserie chickens can be a great protein base for many dishes. (Yes, chefs buy them too!) And if you want to get a great, hearty meal on the table quickly, this is a good way to save time.

Everyone loves potpies, but ones you can pick up in your hand are fun, kid-friendly, and ideal for trips to the arena. If you're pressed for time, store-bought pie crust dough is perfectly acceptable.

The chicken salad dish is a healthy gluten-free alternative to sandwiches and adds a nutritional punch while lowering the carb count. It makes an elegant meal for lunch. But if you want to make this more into a party recipe, set it up like a taco bar with vegetables, hot sauce, and garnishes like fresh herbs.

Rotisserie chicken paired with the wonderful medley of earthy spices, fresh herbs, and vibrant pomegranate seeds in the wraps makes for lively lunch fare that is complex in flavor yet deceptively easy to make.

Serves 4

1

Chicken Hand Pies

3 Tbsp butter
1 small white onion, finely chopped
½ small carrot, finely chopped
½ stalk celery, finely chopped
1 cup shredded rotisserie chicken
1 Tbsp finely chopped thyme
2 Tbsp all-purpose flour, plus extra for dusting (divided)
1 cup chicken stock
¼ cup milk
¼ cup frozen peas
Salt and pepper, to taste
1 quantity Pie Crust Dough (page 197)
1 egg, beaten with 1 Tbsp cold water

Preheat the oven to 400°F. Line a baking sheet with parchment paper.

In a medium saucepan over medium heat, melt butter. Add onions, carrots, and celery and sauté for 10–12 minutes, until softened. Add chicken and thyme and sauté for another 3–5 minutes, until heated through.

Add 2 Tbsp flour and stir to coat the vegetables. Pour in chicken stock and milk and stir until smooth and lump-free. Bring to a boil. Reduce heat to medium-low and simmer for 5 minutes, until thickened. Add peas and simmer for another 2–3 minutes. Season with salt and pepper. Set aside to cool completely.

Roll out dough on a lightly floured surface to a ⅛-inch thickness. Using a 4-inch round cookie cutter, cut out 8 rounds. Place 2–3 spoonfuls of cooled chicken mixture into the center of each round.

Gently fold the round over to form a half-moon shape. Brush edges with egg wash and, using your fingers or a fork, crimp edges to seal. Cut a small opening on the top of each pie (to release steam during baking) and brush the tops with egg wash.

Bake for 20–25 minutes, until golden brown. Place 2 hand pies each onto 4 plates and serve.

2

Chicken Salad Cups

2 cups shredded rotisserie chicken
1 stalk celery, finely chopped
1 scallion, finely sliced
¼ cup mayonnaise
1 tsp lemon juice
Salt and pepper, to taste
1 head Bibb lettuce, leaves separated
1 Tbsp finely chopped parsley, to garnish

In a small bowl, combine chicken, celery, scallion, mayonnaise, lemon juice, and salt and pepper and mix well. Spoon the mixture into lettuce cups, sprinkle with chopped parsley, and serve.

VARIATIONS:

1 Waldorf Salad Add 3 Tbsp chopped walnuts and 1 cup sliced seedless grapes (any kind).

2 Caribbean Salad Replace mayonnaise with the juice from 1 small lime and 1 Tbsp olive oil. Cut 1 small mango into matchsticks and add to mixture. Replace the parsley with 1–2 Tbsp chopped cilantro.

3

Persian Chicken Wrap with Pomegranate Sauce

Persian chicken
2 cups chopped rotisserie chicken
½ small white onion, finely chopped (about ½ cup)
1 Tbsp extra virgin olive oil
1 tsp finely chopped garlic
½ tsp lemon zest
2 Tbsp lemon juice
½ tsp ground cumin
½ tsp ground coriander
¼ tsp cayenne pepper
Salt and pepper, to taste
4 (8-inch) flour tortillas, warmed
½ cup walnuts, coarsely chopped

Torshi
½ small carrot, shredded
2 Tbsp thinly sliced basil
1 Tbsp thinly sliced mint
½ cup iceberg lettuce, shredded
¼ cup baby spinach, thinly sliced
2 Tbsp rice vinegar
1 Tbsp granulated sugar
Salt and pepper, to taste

Dipping sauce
½ cup pomegranate juice
1 Tbsp granulated sugar
¼ tsp finely chopped garlic
Pinch of salt and pepper
2 Tbsp lemon juice
1 Tbsp finely chopped parsley
1 Tbsp thinly sliced mint

To make the chicken, in a bowl, combine chicken, onions, oil, garlic, lemon zest and juice, and spices. Mix well. Season with salt and pepper and set aside.

To make the torshi, in a small bowl, combine carrot, basil, mint, lettuce, and spinach. In a small bowl, combine vinegar and sugar and mix well. Pour over the lettuce mixture. Season with salt and pepper and set aside.

To make the dipping sauce, in a small saucepan over medium heat, combine pomegranate juice, sugar, garlic, and salt and pepper. Simmer for 2 minutes. Set aside to cool slightly. Add lemon juice, parsley, and mint. Set aside.

Divide chicken mixture and torshi among 4 tortillas. Sprinkle walnuts overtop and serve with dipping sauce.

Curried Chicken Salad Tiffin Tin

Let me introduce you to the new lunch box. Commonly used in South Asia, tiffin tins are complete and portable lunches, served warm or hot, in stacked metal containers that lock together. When I began experimenting with versions of the tiffin tin at the Westin Harbour Castle in Toronto, they became on overnight success.

I'm asked to make them a few times a month, and this version marries Indian flavors and typical lunch fare. Tiffin tins are available in most kitchen supply stores or large Asian markets and online.

To make the fruit salad, in a bowl, combine all ingredients. Set aside.

To make the chicken salad, in a sealed container or resealable plastic bag, combine chicken, shallot, garlic, lemon juice, olive oil, thyme, and salt and pepper. Refrigerate overnight.

Preheat the oven to 400°F.

Place marinated chicken in a small baking dish and roast for 18–20 minutes, until chicken is cooked through and the internal temperature reaches 165°F. Set aside to cool completely.

Dice the breasts into ¼-inch pieces. In a large bowl, combine chicken and dressing ingredients. Mix well. Refrigerate until ready to use.

To serve, place fruit salad into bottom compartment, naan (or tortillas), lettuce, and sliced tomatoes into the middle, and curried chicken salad into top.

VARIATION:

1 **Gluten-Free Lettuce Wraps** Replace naan or tortillas with 4 large butter lettuce leaves.

Serves 4

Fruit salad
1 mango, peeled and chopped
1 orange, peeled and segmented
1 cup strawberries, hulled and quartered
1 cup chopped pineapple
1 cup chopped honeydew or cantaloupe melon
½ cup blackberries

Chicken salad
1 lb boneless, skinless chicken breast
1 shallot, finely chopped
1 clove garlic, finely chopped
2 Tbsp lemon juice
2 tsp olive oil
½ tsp chopped thyme
Pinch of salt and pepper
4 naan or small (6-inch) tortillas, cut in half and wrapped individually in waxed paper, to serve
4 large leaves green leaf lettuce, to serve
2 large tomatoes, sliced, to serve

Dressing
½ cup mayonnaise
2 tsp mango chutney
2 dashes Tabasco sauce
1 Tbsp curry powder
Pinch of ground cinnamon
½ tsp ground cumin
Pinch of cayenne pepper
¼ tsp ground coriander
Salt and pepper, to taste
¼ cup diced Granny Smith apples, skin on
¼ cup chopped celery

Ploughman's Lunch Three Ways

During spring and summer on my parents' farm, field work was a top priority. While lunch was a necessity, our lunch hours were limited. For me, food tastes better when you're sitting in a field under blue skies. I have fond memories of sharing meals with my dad where we sat on the ground next to the parked combine, tractor, or hay baler, eating packed lunches known as ploughman's lunch. Modern interpretations often resemble a rustic version of on-the-go charcuterie, cheese, and antipasto platters.

Serves 4

Traditional

4 (3 × 6-inch) slices sourdough bread
¼ cup Boursin cheese, softened
¼ cup Branston Pickle
1 small head radicchio
6 oz cooked ham, sliced
½ cup gherkins
4 oz aged cheddar cheese or Guinness cheddar cheese, thinly sliced
1 large Granny Smith apple, thinly sliced

Salt cod brandade

4 (¾-inch-thick) slices pumpernickel bread, halved
¼ cup softened cream cheese
2 cups Brandade (page 197)
2 cups watercress
2 large tomatoes, each cut into 8 wedges
1 bunch white radishes, washed and trimmed, cut into quarters
1 large bunch seedless grapes

Pickled onions and boiled egg

8 (½-inch-thick) slices baguette, toasted
4 tsp grainy mustard
8 leaves butter lettuce
1 cup canned pimiento peppers, drained and chopped
8 boiled eggs, peeled and sliced into rounds
4 (1-oz) pieces Brie cheese
1 cup Pickled Red Onions (page 61)
4 sprigs flat-leaf parsley
8 strawberries

THE MAIN ATTRACTION

As the adage goes, we are what we eat. Farmers know this intimately. On our farm, we raised more than 100 cattle and dozens of chickens and pigs each year, and I learned to respect and appreciate the value of these animals. My mother was a thrifty cook who adopted the head to tail concept long before it was ever a movement. She carefully organized the freezer and arranged the cuts of meat so that our kitchen was set up for year-round success.

Charlene and I are both from Western Canada and enjoy Alberta Beef. When we first started dating, I surprised her with an incredible dining experience. I converted her tiny apartment into a five-star dining room and served an herb-and-butter-basted beef steak as the main course. Some of the most thoroughly satisfying dishes can be uncomplicated, yet full of flavor, and I encourage you to discuss your options with your local butcher or fishmonger. A luxurious soul-warming Osso Buco with Gremolata page 112 or Beer-Braised Beef Stew page 128 proves that superbly satisfying dishes can be created by coaxing flavor out of cheaper cuts of meat. Moreover, easy-cook recipes—from quick Stress-Free Meals page 132 to delicious Spatchcock Chicken page 116—are guaranteed to make feasting simple.

A main doesn't always require a trip to the butcher. On a lighter side of things, Blackened Halibut with Warm Tomato Bruschetta page 119 and Crispy Trout with Green Beans, Almonds, and Sherry Vinaigrette page 124 will appeal to even the most discerning pescatarians. A vegetarian-friendly recipe such as Stuffed Squash with Spiced Lentils, Chickpeas, and Olives page 115 can be a hearty affair without weighing you down.

Osso Buco
with Gremolata

Serves 4

Osso buco
½ cup all-purpose flour
½ Tbsp salt, plus extra to taste
½ Tbsp black pepper, plus extra
  to taste
4 large lamb, beef, or veal shanks
3 Tbsp olive oil
1 cup pearl onions
1 cup chopped carrots
1 cup red or white wine (red wine
  adds a nice color, but white wine
  is traditional)
2 cloves garlic, chopped
1 Tbsp tomato paste
½ cup diced tomatoes
4 cups beef or chicken stock
2 sprigs thyme
2 bay leaves

Gremolata
Zest of 1 lemon
1 clove garlic, finely chopped
¼ cup finely chopped parsley

Osso buco—an Italian dish made with a veal shank that has a marrow-bone in it—is often the most expensive dish on a restaurant menu because of its long preparation time. This slow cooker version maintains all the delight of the original, but uses cheaper cuts (you can substitute lamb for veal).

Gremolata is a condiment made with fresh herbs and lemon and makes the perfect accompaniment to perk up the slow-cooked richness of the osso buco.

To make the osso buco, in a shallow bowl, combine flour, salt, and pepper. Dredge shanks in the mixture, shaking off any excess.

Heat oil in a heavy-bottomed skillet over medium-high heat. Place shanks in the skillet and sear, turning occasionally, for 6 minutes, until golden on all sides. Transfer shanks to a slow cooker.

Heat the same skillet over medium-high heat. Add pearl onions and chopped carrots and cook for 2 minutes. Pour in wine to deglaze, stirring continuously. Add garlic, tomato paste, tomatoes, and stock. Mix well. Pour mixture into the slow cooker.

Add thyme and bay leaves to slow cooker. Season with salt and pepper. Cover and cook on low heat for 6–8 hours, until tender.

Meanwhile, make the gremolata. In a small ramekin, combine all ingredients. Set aside.

Ladle osso buco into shallow serving dishes. Sprinkle gremolata overtop and serve.

VARIATIONS:

 1 Oxtail with Gremolata and Risotto Replace the shanks with oxtail and serve with cooked risotto (page 154).

2 Beef Stew with Gremolata and Creamy Polenta Replace the shanks with stewing beef and serve with polenta (page 55).

Stuffed Squash
with Spiced Lentils, Chickpeas, and Olives

This vegetarian version of a classic Moroccan tagine is cooked in acorn squash. Warm, spicy, and deeply satisfying, this dish boasts a dynamic complexity thanks to the olives, spices, and lentils. Prepare the stew a day ahead to intensify the flavors.

Preheat the oven to 400°F.

Brush olive oil on cut sides of acorn squash and season with salt and pepper.

Place the squash halves, skin-side down, onto a baking sheet and roast for 20 minutes, until tender. Remove from heat and set aside to cool.

While squash is baking, in a large saucepan over medium-high heat, heat oil. Add onions and garlic and sauté for 4 minutes, until onions are softened. Stir in carrots, parsnip, sweet potato, and butternut squash and cook for another 3 minutes. Add red pepper, zucchini, chickpeas, stock (or water), crushed tomatoes, and olives and bring to a boil. Reduce heat to medium-low and simmer, uncovered, for 15 minutes, until vegetables are tender. Stir in lentils and spices and cook for another 15 minutes.

Remove the stew from the heat and adjust seasoning to taste. Stir in parsley and cilantro. Add steamed rice, if using, to each squash half, ladle stew overtop, and serve.

VARIATION:

1 Stuffed Squash with Chickpeas, Dried Fruit, and Halloumi
Replace the olives with chopped dried apricots, dates, or figs and top each acorn stew bowl with grilled halloumi cheese.

Serves 4

1 tsp olive oil
2 large acorn squash, halved lengthwise and seeded
Salt and pepper, to taste
2 Tbsp vegetable oil
1 small onion, finely chopped
2 cloves garlic, finely chopped
1 small carrot, finely chopped
1 small parsnip, finely chopped
1 small sweet potato, peeled and chopped
1 cup peeled, seeded, and chopped butternut squash
1 red bell pepper, seeded and finely chopped
1 small zucchini, finely chopped
1 (15-oz) can chickpeas, drained and rinsed
3 cups vegetable stock or water
2 cups crushed tomatoes
¾ cup pitted Kalamata or black olives
½ cup dry brown lentils, rinsed
1 small cinnamon stick
1½ Tbsp ground coriander
2½ tsp ground cumin
1½ tsp paprika
1 tsp ground turmeric
1 cup chopped parsley, to garnish
½ cup chopped cilantro, to garnish (optional)
1 cup steamed rice, to serve (optional)

Spatchcock Chicken Three Ways

Spatchcock or butterflied chicken is a term used to describe a whole flattened chicken that has had its backbone removed. The even thickness of the bird makes it fast and easy to cook, especially if you use a cast-iron skillet. They can be found easily at major grocery stories, or you can buy a whole chicken and butterfly it at home.

Roast chicken with tangy lemon and earthy, aromatic sage is a family-friendly meal with maximum appeal. The Hungarian version, with paprika and onion, has a distinctive flavor perfect for those autumnal nights when the temperature drops and comfort food is a top priority.

Those who know me know that I'll find any excuse to add curry flavors to a recipe. My version of tandoori chicken is much simpler for a home cook than traditional methods, which require blazing-hot clay ovens.

Serves 4

Chicken with Lemon and Sage

Chicken
1 (3½–4-lb) whole chicken
Salt and pepper, to taste
1 large onion, sliced
2 carrots, chopped
3 stalks celery, chopped
1 lemon, cut into slices
¼ cup chopped parsley

Lemon and sage butter
¼ cup (½ stick) butter, softened
1 lemon, zested and juiced
4 cloves garlic, finely chopped
2 sage leaves, finely chopped
Pinch of red pepper flakes

Preheat the oven to 400°F.

To butterfly the chicken, pat it dry with absorbent towel. Using kitchen utility scissors, cut along one side of the backbone starting from the tail to the neck. Repeat with the other side of the backbone, remove it (discard or reserve it for stock), and place chicken, breast-side up, onto work surface. Using your hands, gently press down on chicken breasts to flatten the bird.

To make the butter, in a small bowl, combine all ingredients. Mix well. Rub chicken with flavored butter and season with salt and pepper.

Heat a large cast-iron skillet over medium-high heat. Place chicken in skillet, skin-side down, and sear for 4 minutes, until golden. Flip and sear for another 4 minutes.

Place onions, carrots, and celery around chicken. Roast for 30–45 minutes, until chicken is cooked through and the internal temperature reaches 165°F. Remove from the oven. Tent with foil to keep warm and set aside to rest for 10–12 minutes.

Transfer chicken to a cutting board and cut into quarters. Arrange chicken and vegetables on a serving platter and top with the sliced lemons and chopped parsley. Pour pan drippings overtop and serve.

2

Paprika and Onion Chicken

Chicken
1 (3½–4-lb) whole chicken
Salt and pepper, to taste
2 large onions, chopped
1 red bell pepper, seeded and chopped
1 green bell pepper, seeded and chopped
1 yellow bell pepper, seeded and chopped
1 cup dry white wine

Rosemary and paprika rub
3 Tbsp vegetable oil
2 Tbsp finely chopped rosemary
3 cloves garlic, finely chopped
2½ Tbsp sweet paprika
1 tsp cumin seeds
Pinch of red pepper flakes

To butterfly the chicken, pat it dry with absorbent towel. Using kitchen utility scissors, cut along one side of the backbone starting from the tail to the neck. Repeat with the other side of the backbone, remove it (discard or reserve it for stock), and place chicken, breast-side up, onto work surface. Using your hands, gently press down on chicken breasts to flatten the bird.

   To make the rub, in a small bowl, combine all ingredients. Mix well. Rub chicken with mixture and season with salt and pepper. Cover with plastic wrap and marinate in the refrigerator for at least 4 hours.

   Preheat the oven to 400°F.

   Set a large cast-iron skillet over medium-high heat. Season chicken with salt and pepper. Place chicken in skillet, skin-side down, and sear for 4 minutes, until golden. Flip and sear for another 4 minutes. Add onions, peppers, and white wine around chicken and roast for 30–45 minutes, until chicken is cooked through and the internal temperature reaches 165°F. Remove from the oven. Tent with foil to keep warm and set aside to rest for 10–12 minutes.

   Transfer chicken to a cutting board and cut into quarters. Arrange chicken on a serving platter and top with roasted onions and peppers. Pour pan drippings overtop and serve.

3

Tandoori Chicken

Chicken
1 (3½–4-lb) whole chicken
Salt and pepper, to taste
4 large naan bread, to serve

Yogurt and tandoori marinade
1 cup plain yogurt
3 Tbsp vegetable oil
3 cloves garlic, chopped
1 small chili, finely chopped
1 Tbsp grated ginger
½ cup chopped cilantro
3 scallions, finely chopped
2 Tbsp store-bought tandoori paste

Side salad
1 large English cucumber, chopped
½ small red onion, sliced
2 large tomatoes, chopped
1 lime, juiced
¼ cup chopped cilantro

To butterfly the chicken, pat it dry with absorbent towel. Using kitchen utility scissors, cut along one side of the backbone starting from the tail to the neck. Repeat with the other side of the backbone, remove it (discard or reserve it for stock), and place chicken, breast-side up, onto work surface. Using your hands, gently press down on chicken breasts to flatten the bird.

   To make the marinade, in a small bowl, combine all ingredients. Mix well. Rub chicken with marinade. Cover with plastic wrap and marinate in the refrigerator for at least 4 hours.

   Preheat the oven to 400°F.

   Set a large cast-iron skillet over medium-high heat. Season chicken with salt and pepper. Place chicken into skillet, skin-side down, and sear for 4 minutes, until golden. Flip and sear for another 4 minutes. Roast for 30–45 minutes, until chicken is cooked through and the internal temperature reaches 165°F. Remove from the oven. Tent with foil to keep warm and set aside to rest for 10–12 minutes.

   In a medium bowl, combine all salad ingredients. Mix well.

   Transfer chicken to a cutting board and cut into quarters and place on a serving platter. Top with cilantro and serve with warm naan bread and the side salad.

Spiced Turkey Patties
with Mango, Cilantro, and Lemon Mayonnaise

Serves 4

Lemon mayonnaise
1 cup mayonnaise
2 Tbsp lemon juice
1 tsp chopped chives
1 tsp chopped dill

Turkey patties
1½ lb raw ground turkey
3 scallions, chopped
¾ cup store-bought mango chutney, puréed
3 Tbsp chopped cilantro
3 Tbsp chopped mint
1 lemon, zested
2 eggs
¼ cup cornmeal
½ tsp red pepper flakes
¼ tsp salt, plus extra to taste
¼ tsp pepper, plus extra to taste
1–2 Tbsp canola oil
Cilantro, to garnish

Ground turkey may seem yawn inducing, but these patties are not. When working with ground meat, it's important to understand that more fat means more flavor. Because turkey is very lean, you need to consider ways of adding fat (like the lemon mayonnaise in this recipe) to brighten up the meat.

To make the lemon mayonnaise, in a small bowl, combine all ingredients. Mix well. Set aside.

To make the turkey patties, in a medium bowl, combine all ingredients, except for oil and cilantro. Mix well. Evenly divide the mixture into 8. Shape into patties about 3 inches in diameter.

Heat a grill pan over medium heat or preheat the barbecue to 350°F. Lightly oil the grill pan or barbecue grates with oil. Place patties in grill pan or on barbecue and cook for 5 minutes. Flip and cook for another 4–5 minutes, until juices run clear and internal temperature reaches 165°F.

Transfer patties to a serving platter. Season with salt and pepper. Set aside to rest for 4 minutes.

Place a small dollop of lemon mayonnaise on each patty. Garnish with a sprig of cilantro and serve.

VARIATIONS:

1 Brunch Patties with Lemon Mayonnaise, Poached Eggs, and Hollandaise Top the patties with poached eggs (page 36) and a dollop of hollandaise sauce.

2 Turkey Sliders Make 16 small patties, cook them for 2–3 minutes on each side, until juices run clear. Place in slider buns and serve as an appetizer or canapé.

Blackened Halibut
with Warm Tomato Bruschetta

Halibut is a firm white fish that takes on spices well. To ramp up the summery flavor, we've added sweet and tangy cherry tomato bruschetta—it also provides a nice balance to the charred fish.

To make the spice blend, in a small bowl, combine Corbin's essential BBQ rub, mustard, smoked paprika, and nutmeg. Mix well. Sprinkle over the halibut.

In a large nonstick skillet or cast-iron grill pan over medium-high heat, heat oil. Add halibut and fry 3 minutes. Flip and fry for another 3 minutes, until cooked through (fish will be firm and flake easily). (Reduce heat if fish begins to darken too much.)

Season fish with salt. Transfer to a plate.

To make the tomato bruschetta, in the same skillet over medium heat, heat oil. Add garlic and scallions and sauté for 1 minute, until fragrant. Add tomatoes and vinegar. Stir and cook for 1 minute, until tomatoes are warm and still retain their shape. Remove from heat.

Place halibut on top of tomatoes. Sprinkle basil overtop. Serve with lemon wedges and a side of steamed rice.

VARIATIONS:

1 **Blackened Salmon with Olives, Capers, and Tomatoes** Replace the halibut with salmon. Add ¼ cup chopped Kalamata olives and ½ Tbsp whole capers with the tomatoes.

2 **Blackened Chicken with Tomatoes and Avocado** Replace the halibut with chicken breasts pounded to a ½-inch thickness and cook accordingly. Serve with sliced avocado.

Serves 4

Blackening spice blend
2 tsp Corbin's Essential BBQ Rub (page 196)
1 tsp ground mustard
1 tsp smoked paprika
Pinch of ground nutmeg
4 (5-oz) halibut pieces, boneless and skinless
2 Tbsp olive oil
Salt, to taste

Tomato bruschetta
1 tsp olive oil
2 cloves garlic, chopped
1 bunch scallions, chopped
2 cups cherry tomatoes, halved
2 Tbsp white wine vinegar
8 basil leaves, torn
4 lemon wedges
Steamed rice, to serve

Cedar-Planked Pork Tenderloin
with Pineapple and Onion Relish

Serves 4

Pineapple and onion relish
1 cup chopped pineapple
½ small red onion, chopped
1 tsp finely chopped jalapeno
2 Tbsp lime juice
3 Tbsp torn basil

Tenderloin
2 (12-oz) pork tenderloins, trimmed
1 large cedar plank, soaked in
     water for 1 hour
Salt and pepper, to taste

Marinade
1 shallot, finely chopped
2 Tbsp grainy mustard
2 Tbsp pure maple syrup
1 Tbsp finely chopped rosemary
1 tsp smoked paprika

Pork tenderloins are readily available and inexpensive boneless cuts of meat. The most challenging part of making a tenderloin is deciding what flavors to pair it with. The combination of cedar, mustard, and maple syrup is a classic, and outdoor barbecue cooking imparts a tremendous depth of flavor.

To make the relish, in a small bowl, combine all ingredients. Mix well. Cover and refrigerate until needed.

To make the tenderloin, in a large resealable plastic bag, combine tenderloins and marinade ingredients. Seal bag and gently turn back and forth to coat pork. Refrigerate for at least 3 hours or overnight.

Preheat the barbecue to 350°F.

Remove tenderloins from bag and place on the grill. Sear on all sides. Transfer tenderloins to the soaked cedar plank. Season with salt and pepper. Put the plank on the grill, close the lid, and cook for 15–20 minutes, or until the pork reaches an internal temperature of 145°F.

Carefully remove the plank from the grill. Cover plank with aluminum foil. Set aside to rest for 5 minutes.

Slice pork into ½-inch-thick medallions and serve with pineapple and onion relish.

VARIATIONS:

1 **Cedar-Planked Salmon and Shrimp** Replace the pork tenderloin with 1 lb Atlantic salmon fillets and 12 poached shrimp.

2 **Cedar-Planked Pork Tenderloin with Tomato, Jalapeno, and Cilantro Relish** Replace the pineapple with 1 large tomato and add ½ tsp diced jalapeno and 1 tsp chopped cilantro.

3 **Cedar-Planked Tenderloin in Lettuce Cups** Slice the cooked pork tenderloin, add to large lettuce cups, and top with pineapple relish.

Spicy Skillet T-Bone Steak

A T-bone steak is the best of both worlds: strip loin and fillet. This delicious recipe is a great one to have in your back pocket when the weather doesn't cooperate with your barbecue plans. The cast-iron pan is key to having that beautiful crust. (It's the secret that steakhouses don't want you to know about.)

To make the rub, in a spice mill, combine all ingredients and grind until coarse. (Alternatively, use a pestle and mortar.)

To make the steak, rub the blend on both sides of the steaks. In a large cast-iron skillet over high heat, heat oil until it begins to smoke. Carefully lower steaks into skillet and sear for 4 minutes, flipping frequently, until dark golden on both sides. Add butter and baste steaks, taking care not to burn the butter or steaks. (Reduce to medium-high heat if necessary.) Cook for another 3 minutes for medium-rare (when internal temperature reaches 120–125°F).

Transfer steaks to plates. Set aside to rest for 5 minutes. Slice and serve with Duck Fat Roasted Potatoes or Potato Chip Coins, asparagus, and cauliflower, if using.

VARIATION:

1 **T-Bone Steak with Rosemary, Garlic, and Shallots** Replace the peppercorn spice blend with coarse salt and pepper. Add rosemary (or thyme), 1 clove garlic, chopped, and 1 shallot, chopped, to the skillet with the butter.

Serves 4

Rub
½ small cinnamon stick
1½ tsp black peppercorns
1½ tsp coriander seeds
1½ tsp cumin seeds
1½ tsp mustard seeds
½ tsp cloves
½ tsp fennel seeds
4 cardamom pods, seeds only
1½ tsp coarse sea salt

Steak
2 (16-oz) T-bone steaks, rested at room temperature for 30 minutes
2 Tbsp vegetable oil
3½ Tbsp butter
Duck Fat Roasted Potatoes (page 142) or Potato Chip Coins with Feta Cheese, Olives, and Oregano (page 150), to serve (optional)
Grilled asparagus, to serve (optional)
Roasted cauliflower, to serve (optional)

En Papillote Three Ways

Cooking *en papillote*—a French term for cooking something inside a parchment-paper pouch—allows you to quickly throw together ingredients and bake them in the oven to create a versatile dish. You can even prepare the ingredients and pouch in advance and refrigerate until it's time to cook them.

Traditional Thai recipes—with their long list of ingredients—may intimidate home chefs, but this fast-prep recipe satisfies cravings in less time than it takes to order takeout.

Shrimp marinière is a great dish for fooling people into thinking you went to a lot of trouble.

En papillote cooking also makes steaming vegetables an easy and flavorful affair and ensures you still get your nutrition when you're rushed off your feet. The vegetables come out cooked, flavorful, and coated in their own sauce. This recipe is a favorite of my sons, who have fun helping stuff the pouches.

Serves 4

1

Thai Chicken with Coconut, Ginger, and Peppers

½ cup coconut milk
1 Tbsp lime juice
1 tsp Thai red curry paste
4 (4–6-oz) boneless, skinless chicken breasts,
    cut into strips
½ red bell pepper, seeded and cut into matchsticks
½ yellow bell pepper, seeded and cut into
    matchsticks
½ small red onion, cut into matchsticks
3 thin slices ginger
Salt and pepper, to taste
3 scallions, thinly sliced
2 cups long-grain white rice, rinsed and drained
3 cups water
¼ cup chopped cilantro leaves and stems
4 lime wedges

Preheat the oven to 425°F. Cut parchment paper into 4 (12-inch) squares.

In a small bowl, combine coconut milk, lime juice, and curry paste. Set aside.

Lay squares side-by-side on the counter. Place chicken strips in the center of each square. Top each with peppers, onions, and ginger. Season with salt and pepper. Pour 2 Tbsp of coconut milk mixture over each and top with scallions.

Fold the parchment paper in half over the chicken. Starting from one end, fold and crimp the open edges of the parchment paper together to seal the entire square. Place pouches on baking sheet and bake for 25–30 minutes, until chicken is cooked through and the internal temperature reaches 165°F.

Meanwhile, in a large saucepan over medium-high heat, combine rice and water and bring to a boil. Reduce heat to low. Cover and simmer for 10–15 minutes, until water is absorbed. Set aside for a few minutes.

Remove pouches from the oven. Carefully open pouches and transfer contents to 4 serving plates. Garnish each plate with chopped cilantro and a lime wedge and serve with steamed rice.

2

Shrimp Marinière
with Shallots, Wine, and Garlic

24 (size 31/40) tail-on shrimp, peeled and deveined
2 shallots, finely chopped
8 sprigs thyme
4 bay leaves
2 cloves garlic, finely chopped
3 Tbsp finely chopped parsley (divided)
2 Tbsp butter
Salt and pepper, to taste
1 cup dry white wine
1 loaf crusty bread, to serve

Preheat the oven to 375°F. Cut parchment paper into 4 (12-inch) squares.

Lay squares side-by-side on the counter. Place 6 pieces of shrimp in the center of each square. To each, add some shallots, 2 thyme sprigs, a bay leaf, some garlic, ½ Tbsp chopped parsley, and ½ Tbsp butter. Season with salt and pepper.

Fold the parchment paper in half over shrimp. Starting from one end, fold and crimp the open edges of the parchment paper together, until about 1 inch from the end. Pour in ¼ cup wine and then continue crimping until the entire pouch is sealed. Repeat for remaining pouches. Place pouches on a baking sheet and bake for 15–20 minutes, until shrimp turns pink.

Remove pouches from the oven. Carefully open pouches and transfer contents to 4 serving plates. Garnish each plate with remaining parsley and serve with crusty bread.

3

Lemon-Dressed Vegetable Stacks

12 asparagus, stems trimmed
2 zucchinis, cut into ½-inch rounds
  (36 total)
8 baby bell peppers, in a variety of colors, halved
1 small red onion, sliced into thin rings
2 cloves garlic, finely chopped
1 lemon, zested and juiced
2 Tbsp extra virgin olive oil
3 Tbsp finely chopped parsley (divided)
Salt and pepper, to taste

Preheat the oven to 375°F. Cut parchment paper into 4 (12-inch) squares.

In a large bowl, combine asparagus, zucchinis, peppers, onions, garlic, lemon zest and juice, oil, and 2 Tbsp parsley and season with salt and pepper. Mix well.

Lay squares side-by-side on the counter. In the center of each square, stack 3 zucchini rounds, then 2 baby peppers, another 3 zucchini rounds, and then 1 slice of onion. Stack another 3 zucchini rounds and 3 pieces of asparagus on top.

Fold the parchment paper in half over the vegetables. Starting from one end, fold and crimp the open edges of the parchment paper together until the entire pouch is sealed. Place pouches on baking sheet and bake for 25–30 minutes, until vegetables are tender.

Remove pouches from the oven. Carefully open parchment paper and transfer contents to 4 serving plates. Garnish each plate with the remaining parsley and serve.

Crispy Trout

with Green Beans, Almonds, and Sherry Vinaigrette

Fresh fish doesn't require too much handling to bring out its natural flavor. This trout recipe gives you a professional-level dinner with little effort and time. The key is keeping a close eye on the skin until it crisps because it goes from crisp to burnt very quickly.

To make the sherry vinaigrette, in a small bowl, combine all ingredients and mix well. Set aside.

To make the trout, in a large skillet over medium-high heat, heat oil.

Using paper towels, pat dry the fillets and then season with salt and pepper.

Carefully add fillets to skillet, skin-side down, and cook for 5 minutes. Using a spatula, flip and cook for another 3 minutes. Transfer to a plate.

In the same skillet over medium-high heat, melt butter. Add shallots and garlic and sauté for 2 minutes. Add beans and cook for 4 minutes. Add almonds and cook for 3 minutes, stirring occasionally, until almonds are golden.

Pour the sherry vinaigrette over the green beans. Toss and transfer to a serving platter. Arrange trout, skin-side up, on top of the beans. Serve with fresh squeezed lemons.

VARIATION:

1 Salmon with Asparagus, Almonds, and Sherry Vinaigrette
Replace the trout with 1½ lb salmon and replace the green beans with asparagus or sautéed zucchini.

Serves 4

Sherry vinaigrette
3 Tbsp extra virgin olive oil
1½ Tbsp sherry vinegar
1 tsp honey
Pinch of red pepper flakes
1 lemon, zested
Salt and pepper, to taste

Trout
1 Tbsp olive oil
1 (1-lb) whole trout, cleaned or 4 (6-oz) skin-on trout fillets, pinbones removed
Salt and pepper, to taste
3 Tbsp butter
2 shallots, sliced
2 cloves garlic, chopped
1 lb green beans, trimmed
½ cup slivered almonds
1 lemon, halved

Beer-Braised Beef Stew

Braising—the technique of slow cooking at low temperatures and in high-moisture environments—has the power to transform rustic and simple ingredients into comfort food classics. The combination of stewing beef, hearty root vegetables, and a rich ale-based stock makes for a luxurious, tender, and succulent stew with intriguing undertones.

Preheat the oven to 375°F.

In a shallow baking dish, combine flour, paprika, onion and garlic powders, and salt and pepper. Dredge beef in the mixture, shaking off excess.

In a large Dutch oven over medium-high heat, heat 3 Tbsp oil. Add beef and sear, turning frequently, for 4–5 minutes, until browned on all sides. Transfer to a plate. Set aside.

In the same Dutch oven over medium-high heat, heat remaining 1 Tbsp oil. Add pearl onions and cook for 2 minutes. Add garlic, potatoes, carrots, parsnip, and mushrooms and sauté for 4 minutes. Add beef, tomato paste, bay leaves, thyme, rosemary, ale, and stock. Cover and braise in the oven for 1¼–1½ hours, until meat is tender. Season with salt and pepper

Serve in large serving bowls with a side of homemade biscuits or crusty bread.

VARIATION:

1 Venison Stew with Heirloom Carrots, Celery Root, and Red Wine Replace the beef with venison or lamb. Replace the carrots, parsnip, and mushrooms with 1 cup chopped heirloom carrots and 1 cup chopped celery root. Replace the beer with 1 cup red wine.

Serves 4

1 cup all-purpose flour
1 Tbsp paprika
1 tsp onion powder
1 tsp garlic powder
Salt and pepper, to taste
2 lb stewing beef
4 Tbsp vegetable oil (divided)
1½ cups pearl onions
2 cloves garlic, finely chopped
1½ cups baby potatoes
1 large carrot, chopped
1 large parsnip, chopped
1½ cups cremini mushrooms, cleaned
2 Tbsp tomato paste
2 bay leaves
1 large sprig thyme
1 large sprig of rosemary
2 cups dark ale
2 cups beef stock
Homemade biscuits or crusty bread, to serve

Ground Chicken, Brown Butter, and Sage Gnocchi

Gnocchi is one of those dishes you order in a restaurant that you can't imagine making at home. But the truth is, these soft, pillow-like potato dumplings are easy to make, and once you get the hang of it, they can be made in advance and frozen in resealable bags to pull out later for fuss-free weekday meals.

To make the dough, in a medium pot over high heat, combine Yukon Gold (or yellow) potatoes and enough cold water to cover. Bring to a boil and cook for 30–40 minutes, covered, until potatoes are cooked through. Drain and put the potatoes through a ricer. (Alternatively, use a masher.)

Meanwhile, make the brown butter. In a small saucepan over medium heat, melt butter. Cook for 2–3 minutes, until butter foams and is golden brown. Remove from heat. Using a fine-mesh sieve, strain into a small bowl. Set aside.

To make the gnocchi, place 2½ cups riced (or mashed) potatoes in large bowl. In a medium bowl, combine flour, Parmesan, and nutmeg. Mix well and add to bowl with potatoes. Stir in eggs and season with salt and pepper. Lightly dust a clean work surface with flour. Place dough on the surface and roll into a long cylinder, about ½ inch in diameter. Cut gnocchi into 1-inch pieces. Refrigerate until ready to use.

Bring a large pot of salted water to a boil over high heat. Carefully add gnocchi (working in batches, if necessary, to avoid overcrowding) and cook for 3–4 minutes, until gnocchi float to the surface. Using a slotted spoon, transfer gnocchi to a plate. Set aside.

To make the dish, in a large skillet over medium-high heat, heat oil. Add onions and chicken and sauté for 5 minutes, until chicken is cooked through. Pour in wine and cream and cook for 2 minutes, until reduced by half. Stir in sage and season with salt and pepper. Add gnocchi and gently toss to mix.

Spoon gnocchi into 4 bowls. Drizzle brown butter overtop, sprinkle with grated Parmesan and serve.

VARIATION:-

1 **Gnocchi with Sausage, Spinach, and Blue Cheese** Replace the chicken with Italian sausage meat, replace the Parmesan with crumbled blue cheese and add 1 cup chopped spinach with the sage. For an herb gnocchi, you could also add ½ cup finely chopped parsley to the dough.

Serves 4

Gnocchi dough
4–5 Yukon Gold or yellow potatoes, peeled
1¼ cups all-purpose flour, plus extra for dusting
2 Tbsp grated Parmesan cheese
Pinch of ground nutmeg
1 whole egg
1 egg yolk
Salt and pepper, to taste

Brown butter
¼ cup (½ stick) butter

Gnocchi dish
1½ Tbsp olive oil
½ small onion, finely chopped
8 oz ground chicken
¼ cup dry white wine
½ cup whipping (35%) cream
2 sage leaves, chopped
Salt and pepper, to taste
2 tsp Brown Butter, to serve
½ cup grated Parmesan cheese, to serve

Fennel and Pistachio Crusted Lamb Rack

Lamb may be readily available in shops across Canada, but it's underrated and underused. The next time you're entertaining guests, consider this dish—it's guaranteed to leave guests with a lasting impression. This recipe calls for Frenched lamb, which simply means removing the meat and fat connected to the individual rib bones to create a tidy and elegant finish.

To make the marinade, in a small bowl, combine all ingredients. Mix well. Brush over the lamb racks and marinate in the refrigerator for at least 3–4 hours or overnight.

Preheat the oven to 400°F.

Heat a large ovenproof skillet over medium-high heat. Place racks in skillet (reserving marinade for later) and sear all sides until dark brown. Transfer racks to a cutting board. Set aside to cool for 5 minutes.

To make the pistachio crust, in a small bowl, combine all ingredients. Mix well. Brush both sides of lamb racks with reserved marinade. Sprinkle pistachio mixture on all sides of lamb and gently pat so that crust sticks to lamb. Place lamb back in skillet and roast in the oven for 10–12 minutes, until cooked to medium (internal temperature reaches 140°F). Remove lamb from oven. Tent with foil to keep warm and set aside to rest for 5–10 minutes.

Slice lamb racks into 2-bone portions. Serve with tzatziki sauce, side green salad, and steamed baby potatoes, if using.

VARIATION:

1 **Mushroom Crusted Pork Tenderloin** Replace the lamb racks with trimmed pork tenderloin, replace the pistachios with 1 cup dried mushrooms and add a pinch of cayenne pepper to the crust mixture.

Serves 4

Marinade
¼ cup extra virgin olive oil
1 Tbsp Dijon mustard
2 shallots, finely chopped
1 clove garlic, finely chopped
½ tsp black pepper
3 Tbsp pure maple syrup

Lamb rack
2 (1-lb) lamb racks, trimmed and Frenched
Tzatziki sauce, to serve (optional)
Side green salad, to serve (optional)
Steamed baby potatoes, to serve (optional)

Pistachio crust
¾ cup pistachio nuts, toasted and crushed
1 Tbsp fennel seeds, toasted and crushed
1½ tsp cumin seeds, toasted and crushed
Salt and pepper, to taste

Stress-Free Meals Three Ways

When you've got to get food on the table fast, it can be a challenge to come up with new and inventive ways to prepare fresh and easy weeknight meals. These family favorites are all about getting good crowd-pleasing grub on the table fast so everyone can gather and have fun.

Bucatini (spaghetti with a hole running through it) is ideal for people who love pasta sauce because each strand can hold almost its weight in sauce. (Translated for kids: it's great for slurping!) The briny capers and meaty olives add savory depths—perfect for vegetarians, flexitarians, or those wanting to cut back on meat. For a boost of umami, try adding anchovies to this dish.

Chilaquiles come from humble ingredients. If your kids can eat salsa, they're going to love these. You don't have to travel south of the border to get authentic Mexican food.

If there's one piece of kitchen gear that I can truly not live without, it's my reliable cast-iron Dutch oven. Golden roast chicken, savory soppressata, and fresh herbs make an instant classic of this truly satisfying and soothing rigatoni dish.

Serves 4

1

Bucatini with Onions, Capers, and Olives

½ lb bucatini pasta
1 small onion, finely chopped
2 cloves garlic, finely chopped
½ cup black olives, pitted
½ cup capers
1 tsp anchovy paste (optional)
1 pint cherry tomatoes, halved
4 cups chicken stock
3 Tbsp basil, thinly sliced (divided)
1 tsp red pepper flakes
2 Tbsp extra virgin olive oil
Salt and pepper, to taste
Grated Parmesan cheese, to serve

In a large saucepan, combine pasta, onions, garlic, black olives, capers, anchovy paste, if using, cherry tomatoes, chicken stock, 2 Tbsp basil, red pepper flakes, and olive oil. Bring to a boil over high heat. Cover, reduce heat to a simmer and cook for 10–15 minutes, stirring frequently, until pasta is al dente (tender but still a little firm to the bite) and most of the chicken stock has been absorbed.

Remove from the heat. Season with salt and pepper. Spoon pasta onto 4 plates and sprinkle with remaining basil and the Parmesan cheese.

Chilaquiles

Salsa verde
8 tomatillos, husked and rinsed
½ white onion, coarsely chopped
2 cloves garlic
1 jalapeno, seeded, stem removed
¼ cup low-sodium chicken stock
Salt and pepper, to taste

Chilaquiles
12 (6-inch) corn tortillas
2 cups canola oil
2 eggs, beaten
Salt and pepper, to taste
½ cup shredded Monterey Jack cheese

Garnish
2 Tbsp queso fresco (or mild feta cheese), crumbled
2 white onions, finely chopped
2 Tbsp finely chopped cilantro
¼ cup sour cream
1 avocado, pitted, peeled and cut into ½-inch cubes

To make the salsa verde, in a medium saucepan, combine tomatillos, onions, garlic, and jalapeno. Add enough water to cover and bring to a boil over medium-high heat. Reduce heat to low and simmer for 15–20 minutes, until vegetables are tender and tomatillos are pale. Set aside to cool slightly.

Pour mixture into a blender and purée until smooth. Add chicken stock and season with salt and pepper. Return salsa verde to the saucepan and simmer over medium heat for 15 minutes, until slightly thickened.

Meanwhile, make the chilaquiles. Stack the tortillas and cut into 8 wedges. In a large saucepan over medium-high heat, heat oil until it reaches 350°F. Carefully add tortilla wedges (working in batches, if necessary, to avoid overcrowding) and fry for 1–2 minutes, until golden brown. Using a slotted spoon, transfer chips to a plate lined with paper towels. Set aside.

Increase heat of salsa verde to medium-high. When it starts to bubble, stir in beaten eggs and cook for a few seconds until incorporated. Quickly add tortilla chips and stir mixture until chips have softened. Season with salt and pepper and sprinkle Monterey Jack cheese overtop.

Divide chilaquiles among 4 plates. Sprinkle each plate with queso fresco, onions, and cilantro. Add a dollop of sour cream and avocado and serve warm.

3

Baked Rigatoni with Chicken, Sausage, and Olives

2 Tbsp extra virgin olive oil (divided)
1 small white onion, finely chopped
2 cloves garlic, finely chopped
1 red bell pepper, seeded and cut into matchsticks
1 cup cooked chicken, shredded
1 cup dried sausage, such as soppressata, sliced
½ cup Kalamata olives, pitted
1 tsp finely chopped oregano
1 tsp finely chopped thyme
1 (24-oz) jar tomato sauce
3 cups rigatoni pasta
4 Tbsp basil, thinly sliced (divided)
Salt and pepper, to taste
½ cup ricotta cheese
½ cup grated Parmesan cheese
1 cup grated mozzarella cheese

Preheat the oven to 400°F.

In a large saucepan over medium-high heat, heat 1 Tbsp oil. Add onions and sauté for 3 minutes, until softened and translucent. Add garlic and sauté for 2–3 minutes, until fragrant. Add peppers and sauté for 3–4 minutes, until softened.

Add chicken, sausage, olives, oregano, thyme, and tomato sauce. Bring to a boil, then reduce heat to low and simmer for 15 minutes.

Meanwhile, make the pasta. Bring a large saucepan of salted water to a boil over high heat. Add pasta and cook for 12–15 minutes, until al dente (tender but still a little firm to the bite). Drain pasta and toss with remaining 1 Tbsp oil (to prevent noodles from sticking together).

Remove sauce from the heat. Stir in 2 Tbsp basil, and season with salt and pepper. Ladle half the sauce into a 9 × 13-inch ovenproof dish. Add half the ricotta in an even layer, and then the pasta in an even layer. Pour remaining sauce over pasta, add remaining ricotta in an even layer, and sprinkle Parmesan and mozzarella overtop. Bake for 10–15 minutes, until the cheese is melted and golden.

To serve, spoon pasta onto 4 plates and garnish with remaining basil.

MATTER
OF
SIDES

Side dishes have really evolved over the past few years.
These days, whenever I visit my grocer or farmer's market,
I marvel at the spectrum of fresh, wholesome crops.
Vegetables that have been picked at the height of the season
are capable of delivering intense flavor with minimal effort.
Whether they're bright, dynamic, complementary dishes
to mains, creative tapas, or even mini meals on their own,
accompaniments are at the heart of every meal I cook.

I am incredibly fortunate to live in multicultural Toronto,
where the communities are a constant source of inspiration
for dishes. Family favorites such as the Harissa-Grilled
Broccoli Steaks page 138, Miso and Sake Glazed Japanese
Eggplant with Scallions and Sesame Seeds page 143, or
Potato Chip Coins with Feta Cheese, Olives, and Oregano
page 150 might not exist were it not for my daily interactions
with so many different people and cultures.

And when it comes to trying new dishes—of the vegetable
sort—children may be skeptical and reluctant. My sons
are more likely to try something familiar, so if I'm serving
cauliflower with cheese, I tell them it's "like mac and cheese."
They become fairly adventuresome eaters this way.

Candied Beets
with Maple Syrup and Chives

Serves 2–4

4 baby red beets
4 baby striped beets
4 baby yellow/golden beets
2 Tbsp butter
2 Tbsp brown sugar
1 Tbsp pure maple syrup
Salt and pepper, to taste
½ bunch finely chopped chives

Beets bring back memories of being in my mother's kitchen in the late summer, peeling and canning beets for winter dinners. They also happen to be the cornerstone of borscht (page 77), one of my all-time favorite dishes.

While red beets are perfectly suited for this recipe, take advantage of the many summertime varieties for a thoroughly inspired dish— they look like gorgeous jewels on a plate and with this particular recipe, they taste as good as they look.

In a large pot over medium-high heat, combine beets and enough cold water to cover. Bring to a boil and cook, covered, for 45–60 minutes, until beets are tender and can be easily pierced with a knife. Remove from the heat. Peel beets under running water, and cut in half.

In a large skillet over medium-high heat, melt butter. Add brown sugar and maple syrup and simmer for 5 minutes, until golden and syrupy. Add beets and cook for 5 minutes, until most of sauce has evaporated and beets begin to caramelize. Remove from heat. Season with salt and pepper.

Sprinkle chives overtop and toss. Transfer to a serving platter and serve warm.

VARIATION:

1 **Candied Carrots and Parsnip** Replace beets with an equal amount of carrots and parsnips.

Harissa-Grilled Broccoli Steaks

Serves 4

2 heads broccoli
1 Tbsp extra virgin olive oil
Salt and pepper, to taste
2 Tbsp harissa

As plant-based diets grow in popularity, chefs around the world are looking for more innovative ways to use vegetables. Harissa— a North African spice blend that can be found at large supermarkets— adds a heat and savory bite to vegetables and makes a great counter- point to the slightly sweet flavor of grilled broccoli.

Heat a grill pan over medium heat or preheat the barbecue to 350°F.

Starting at the stem, cut each broccoli head in half and then cut each half in half again. In a large bowl, combine broccoli and oil and season with salt and pepper. Toss to mix.

Place broccoli in the grill pan or on the barbecue and cook 4 minutes. Turn 45 degrees, then grill for another 4–5 minutes, until nicely charred and cooked through.

Transfer broccoli to a serving bowl. Sprinkle harissa overtop. Toss to mix and serve.

VARIATION:

1 Harissa-Grilled Baby Bok Choy Replace the broccoli with 8 baby bok choy halved lengthwise.

Grilled Fennel and Mushrooms
with Tarragon Vinaigrette

Serves 4

Grilled vegetables
2 fennel bulbs
4 cups cremini mushrooms,
   cleaned and quartered
1 Tbsp olive oil
Salt and pepper, to taste

Tarragon vinaigrette
2 tsp Dijon mustard
¼ cup red wine vinegar
4–6 Tbsp extra virgin olive oil
Honey, to taste
Salt and pepper, to taste
2 sprigs tarragon, finely chopped

This is a dish that looks beautiful and tastes great—the sweet fennel contrasts with the earthy mushrooms, and the vinaigrette wakes up all the flavors on the plate.

When entertaining, it's important to always be aware of how much total work you have to do to put a meal together. Having some easier recipes in your repertoire that still deliver great flavor is an easy way to make your home kitchen more like a professional kitchen, where every minute counts.

To make the grilled vegetables, heat a grill pan over medium heat or preheat the barbecue to 350°F.

Cut fennel bulbs in quarters, remove the core and then cut crosswise into ½-inch slices. In a medium bowl, combine fennel, mushrooms, and oil and season with salt and pepper. Toss to mix.

Place fennel and mushrooms in grill pan or on barbecue and cook, flipping halfway to ensure even cooking on all sides, until nicely charred and cooked through, about 10–12 minutes for the fennel and 6–8 minutes for the mushrooms. (If using a grill pan, grill fennel for 4 minutes, then rotate fennel 45 degrees. Add mushrooms and grill for another 6–8 minutes, flipping midway through grilling to ensure even cooking on all sides.) Remove from grill and place on a serving platter.

To make the tarragon vinaigrette, in a medium bowl, combine mustard and vinegar and whisk. While whisking, slowly pour in the oil until emulsified. Whisk in honey and salt and pepper. Stir in chopped tarragon.

Drizzle vinaigrette over the grilled vegetables and serve.

Roasted Sweet Potatoes
with Onion, Dill, and Caraway Seeds

Serves 4

3 sweet potatoes or yams, peeled
    and sliced
½ small white onion, thinly sliced
2 Tbsp extra virgin olive oil
2 Tbsp caraway seeds, toasted
Salt and pepper, to taste
6 sprigs dill, chopped

Onions, dill, and caraway seeds give flavor to a lot of Polish dishes. The twist with this dish is applying those flavors to a vegetable you don't often find on a Polish menu: sweet potato. This recipe is very easy to make but feels like a restaurant quality side thanks to a punch of anise flavor from the caraway seeds.

Preheat the oven to 425°F.

In a large bowl, combine sweet potatoes (or yams), onions, oil, and caraway seeds, and season with salt and pepper. Mix well.

Spread mixture on a baking sheet and roast for 30–40 minutes, until lightly browned and tender. Season with salt and pepper.

Transfer sweet potatoes to a serving platter. Garnish with chopped dill and serve.

Duck Fat Roasted Potatoes

Serves 4

8–10 small Yukon Gold potatoes, peeled and halved
¾ cup duck fat
1½ cups all-purpose flour
Salt and pepper, to taste

Between childhood and culinary school, I've probably prepped enough potatoes to feed an army battalion. People love potatoes because of their versatility and ability to take on just about any seasoning imaginable. Anthea Turner, my co-star on *Dinner Party Wars*, taught me how to make this irresistible recipe. I thought I knew how to roast potatoes until she showed me otherwise. Duck fat can be found at butcher shops and some supermarkets. (See image on page 123.)

Preheat the oven to 400°F.

In a large pot over medium-high heat, combine potatoes and enough cold water to cover potatoes by an inch. Bring to a boil. Reduce heat to medium-low and simmer, covered, for 10–12 minutes, until half cooked (potatoes can be easily pierced by a knife).

Meanwhile, place the duck fat in a heavy-bottomed roasting pan and heat in the oven for 5 minutes.

Drain potatoes and return them to the pot. Add flour and shake the pot, until potatoes are coated.

Remove roasting pan from the oven and add potatoes. Season with salt and pepper and shake potatoes to coat. Roast, uncovered, for 25–30 minutes, tossing halfway through to ensure even cooking, until crisp and golden.

Place potatoes on a large serving platter and serve immediately.

Miso and Sake Glazed Japanese Eggplant
with Scallions and Sesame Seeds

Serves 4

2 small Japanese eggplants,
    washed, halved lengthwise
Salt and pepper, to taste
2 Tbsp vegetable oil
¼ cup miso paste
2 Tbsp mirin
1 Tbsp granulated sugar
1 Tbsp sake
2 Tbsp sesame seeds

This recipe is an homage to my friends from Holt Renfrew: Kaz, Kiku, Katsuyo, Chiharu, Satomi, and Mariko. Eggplant is one of those polarizing vegetables that some people dislike because they've had a negative experience with it. But this versatile dish, with its marriage of classic Japanese flavors and sweet, salty, and umami notes, will appeal to the most discerning foodies.

Preheat the broiler to high heat.

Score the inside of eggplants and season with salt and pepper.

In a skillet over medium-high heat, heat oil. Add eggplants, skin-side down, and cook for 4 minutes, until golden brown. Flip, cover, and cook for another 3–4 minutes, until tender.

Meanwhile, in a small bowl, combine miso, mirin, sugar, and sake and mix well.

Place eggplant, cut-side down, on a baking sheet and spoon on miso mixture so that it covers entire eggplant. Broil for 3–4 minutes, until miso mixture is bubbling. Sprinkle eggplant with sesame seeds and serve immediately.

VARIATION:

1 **Miso Glazed Tofu and Gai Lan** Replace the eggplant with ½ lb firm tofu, cut into 4 equal pieces, and ½ lb gai lan.

Sesame and Chili Roasted Green Beans

Serves 4

1 lb green beans, trimmed
1 Tbsp extra virgin olive oil
Salt and pepper, to taste
1 clove garlic, finely chopped
2 tsp honey
½ tsp sesame oil
¼ tsp red pepper flakes or ½ Tbsp
* thinly sliced fresh chilies*
Pinch of ground ginger
4 tsp toasted sesame seeds

When I was a kid, one of my summer jobs in my mother's kitchen was to trim hundreds of beans for dinner. To me, the snap of a bean is a sound of summer. Roasting these spectacular green beans draws out their natural sweetness,

Preheat the oven to 450°F.

In a medium bowl, combine beans, olive oil, and salt and pepper. Toss to mix. Spread beans on a baking sheet and roast for 8 minutes.

Meanwhile, in a small bowl, combine garlic, honey, sesame oil, red pepper flakes, and ginger and mix well. Drizzle sauce over beans and toss to mix. Roast for another 2 minutes. Season with salt and pepper.

Transfer the beans to a serving platter. Sprinkle toasted sesame seeds overtop and serve.

VARIATION:

1 Sesame and Chili Roasted Asparagus Replace the beans with 2 bunches of trimmed asparagus.

Allspice, Cumin, and Chili Pan-Roasted Brussels Sprouts

Serves 4

1 lb Brussels sprouts, cleaned,
   trimmed, and outer leaves
   removed, halved
2 tsp extra virgin olive oil
1 clove garlic, finely chopped
½ tsp ground cumin
¼ tsp ground allspice
1 tsp red pepper flakes
Salt and pepper, to taste

Brussels sprouts used to be a form of "punishment" when I was a kid, but these days, they are on menus just about everywhere. Roasted Brussels sprouts have a malty flavor that's perfectly matched with this warm, wintry seasoning.

Preheat the oven to 425°F.

In a medium bowl, combine all ingredients except salt and pepper and mix well. Spread on a baking sheet and roast for 20 minutes, until tender. Season with salt and pepper. Serve immediately.

VARIATION:

1 Allspice, Cumin, and Chili Pan-Roasted Turnips with Bacon
Add 6 strips bacon, chopped, and replace the Brussels sprouts with 1 lb baby turnips.

Butter Pecan Butternut Squash

Serves 4

1 large butternut squash (or any
    squash or pumpkin), peeled,
    seeded and cut in quarters
1 Tbsp extra virgin olive oil
Salt and pepper, to taste
1 Tbsp butter
2 Tbsp maple syrup
2 Tbsp brown sugar
½ tsp ground cinnamon
1 cup whole pecans, lightly toasted

The American south is famed for their side dishes—there is no other place on earth that can transform humble vegetables into the ultimate comfort food like they do. In this instance, flavors that ordinarily work together in desserts are put together in a savory side that complements meat dishes such as pork. Even the fussiest child will be charmed by this tasty dish.

Preheat the oven to 400°F.

Place squash (or pumpkin) on baking sheet. Drizzle oil overtop, season with salt and pepper and roast for 30–40 minutes, or until softened.

In a small bowl, combine butter, maple syrup, brown sugar, and cinnamon and mix well. Using a spoon, spread mixture over the squash and sprinkle with pecans. Roast for another 6–8 minutes, until golden and caramelized. Serve immediately.

Garlic Mushrooms
with Rosemary and Salted Pine Nuts

Serves 4

5½ cups mixed mushrooms such as button and cremini, quartered
4 cloves garlic, 2 cloves finely chopped
2 Tbsp + 1 tsp extra virgin olive oil (divided)
1 Tbsp butter
Salt and pepper, to taste
2 Tbsp pine nuts or hazelnuts
1 Tbsp finely chopped rosemary

Earthy mushrooms are often thought of as a side dish, but they can easily take center stage with the right accompaniments. This intensely flavored recipe requires only a few simple yet aromatic ingredients to stand out. It reminds me of those mushroom dishes served at old-fashioned steakhouses, but with a far tastier result.

Preheat the oven to 425°F.

In a medium bowl, combine mushrooms, chopped garlic, 2 Tbsp olive oil, butter, and salt and pepper. Spread on a baking sheet and roast for 15–20 minutes, until mushrooms are cooked through.

Meanwhile, in a small skillet over medium-high heat, heat 1 tsp oil. Add pine nuts (or hazelnuts) and toast for 3–5 minutes, until fragrant and browned. Remove from heat. Add rosemary and season with salt and pepper.

Transfer mushrooms to a serving platter. Add pine nut mixture and toss to mix. Serve immediately.

Potato Chip Coins
with Feta Cheese, Olives, and Oregano

Serves 4

1 lb russet potatoes, sliced ¼-inch
   thick
3 Tbsp extra virgin olive oil
2 Tbsp oregano, finely chopped
Salt and pepper, to taste
¼ cup crumbled feta cheese
¼ cup Kalamata or black olives,
   pitted, sliced

My wife, kids, and friends constantly request this summer barbecue recipe, which was inspired by a very Toronto dish: Greek poutine. I take that idea and transform it into a crowd-pleasing side.

Preheat the barbecue to 350°F.

Bring a medium saucepan of water to a boil over high heat. Add the potato slices (working in batches, if necessary, to avoid overcrowding) and cook for 2–3 minutes, until tender but crisp. Drain potatoes and pat dry with paper towels.

Brush both sides of potatoes with olive oil. Sprinkle with oregano and season with salt and pepper. Place on barbecue, cover and cook for 20 minutes, turning occasionally to ensure even cooking, until browned. Remove from heat and place on a large serving platter. Season with salt and pepper.

Sprinkle crumbled feta and sliced black olives overtop of potatoes just before serving.

VARIATION:

1 Whole Baby Carrots with Goat Cheese, Honey, and Thyme
Replace the potatoes with 1 lb baby carrots. Replace the olives and oregano with 1 Tbsp thyme and the feta cheese with ¼ cup goat cheese, and drizzle 1 Tbsp honey overtop.

GRAINS AND MORE

In the past, poor farmers used grains—spelt, barley, rice, wheat—to make lesser cuts of meat go farther and help fuel busy days tilling the fields. Today, ancient grains such as quinoa, bulgur, and farro are more prevalent in restaurants and home kitchens than ever before. And it pleases me to see them in the spotlight—they're an essential source of complex carbohydrates and fiber.

Not only are they wholesome and nutritious, grains are also incredibly versatile. They absorb flavors well and add texture and body to dishes. They can be nutty flavor carriers in everything from Lemon and Mushroom Risotto page 154 to vibrant power bowls such as the Tri-Colored Quinoa with Black Beans, Spicy Vinaigrette, and Parsley page 160. When treated right, grains will leave you wanting more.

As a young apprentice, I once undercooked wild rice for a salad, and the chef was furious. I have never forgotten the lesson: always test your grains. The texture of a grain should not be crunchy, but rather, al dente (slightly firm to the bite). When cooking any grain, I recommend tasting it several times to ensure the perfect consistency and texture. If all the liquid has been absorbed, but it still doesn't taste like your grains are cooked, add more liquid.

Lemon and Mushroom Risotto

When I dine out at Italian restaurants, I often skip pasta altogether and order the risotto. It's a good way to judge a restaurant, as what separates amazing risotto from just good risotto is technique and experience.

Buttery, cheesy, and comforting, risotto is a hit at home with everyone: my sons consider it the rice version of mac and cheese—it also happens to be Charlene's favorite dish (in fact, it may be the reason she agreed to marry me).

In a large skillet over medium-high heat, heat 1 Tbsp olive oil. Add mushrooms and sauté for 3–4 minutes, until golden brown. Add garlic and sauté for another 2 minutes, until fragrant. Transfer to a plate and set aside.

In the same skillet over medium heat, melt 1 Tbsp butter. Add onions and sauté for 5–7 minutes, until softened and translucent. Add rice, stir to coat, and cook for 2 minutes.

Pour in 1 cup stock and simmer for 2–3 minutes, stirring every few seconds, until the liquid is absorbed. Add another cup of stock and repeat until rice is al dente (tender, but still a little firm to the bite), thick, and creamy.

Remove from heat. Add mushrooms, lemon zest and juice, ½ cup of Parmesan cheese, remaining ¼ cup (½ stick) butter, and parsley. Season with salt and pepper.

Sprinkle the remaining ½ cup Parmesan cheese overtop. Drizzle with the remaining 3 Tbsp olive oil, garnish with parsley, and serve immediately.

VARIATIONS:

1 Lemon, Pea, and Cream Cheese Risotto Replace the mushrooms with green peas, and add mint and a dollop of cream cheese.

2 Arancini Put 1 cup flour, 2 eggs, and 1 cup bread crumbs each in separate shallow dishes. Shape cooled risotto into 1½-inch balls. Dip each rice ball into the flour, the egg, and then the bread crumbs. Deep-fry for 3–4 minutes, until golden and crispy.

Serves 4

4 Tbsp extra virgin olive oil (divided)
1 lb cremini mushrooms, chopped
2 cloves garlic, finely chopped
¼ cup (½ stick) plus 1 Tbsp butter (divided)
1 small onion, finely chopped
1¾ cup arborio rice
6 cups vegetable or chicken stock, hot
3 Tbsp extra virgin olive oil
1 large lemon, zested and juiced
1 cup Parmesan cheese, grated (divided)
3 Tbsp finely chopped parsley, plus extra to garnish
Salt and pepper, to taste

Roasted Cauliflower Couscous

Serves 4

1 large cauliflower, cut into florets
1 tsp ground cinnamon
1 tsp ground cumin
1 tsp ground coriander
1 Tbsp extra virgin olive oil
Salt and pepper, to taste
¼ cup sliced almonds
2 Tbsp finely chopped parsley
2 Tbsp finely chopped cilantro
2 Tbsp finely chopped mint
Zest of 1 lemon

Hearty, robust, and nutty cauliflower makes an excellent stand-in for couscous. Plus, this guilt-free dish is packed with nutrients— once you've mastered the basics, it'll be a staple in your repertoire.

Preheat the oven to 350°F. Line a baking sheet with parchment paper.

Using a food processor or blender, pulse the cauliflower florets into coarse grains.

In a medium bowl, combine cauliflower, spices, olive oil, and salt and pepper and mix well. Spread mixture on the prepared baking sheet and roast for 20–30 minutes, until crispy around edges.

Meanwhile, in a small nonstick skillet over medium-high heat, toast almonds for 2 minutes.

Remove cauliflower from oven and set aside to cool slightly. In medium bowl, combine roasted cauliflower, herbs, and lemon zest and mix well. Season with salt and pepper. Sprinkle toasted almonds overtop and serve warm or cold.

VARIATION:

1 Roasted Cauliflower Couscous 2 Replace the cilantro and mint with more parsley, add 2 whole chopped tomatoes, ½ small red onion, and ½ cup crumbled feta cheese.

Grits
with Cheddar and Peppers

Serves 4

Grits
2 cup water
2 cup milk
Pinch of salt
1 cup stone-ground or regular grits
¼ cup whipping (35%) cream
1 cup white cheddar cheese, grated
2 Tbsp butter
Salt and pepper, to taste

Peppers
1 tsp olive oil
2 large bell peppers, any color,
  seeded and sliced
Salt and pepper, to taste

Grits are hard to come by in Canada, which is a real shame for a country that produces an incredible amount of corn. Well-made grits are a sublime experience. If they're made well, you should be able to taste a distinct corn undertone.

To make the grits, in a large saucepan over medium-high heat, combine water, milk, and salt and bring to a boil. Slowly add grits, stirring continuously. Bring back to a boil. Cover and reduce heat to low. Cook for another 30 minutes, stirring occasionally, until porridge-like in consistency. Add more water or milk if necessary.

  Remove from heat. Stir in cream, cheese, and butter. Season with salt and pepper.

  To make the peppers, in a skillet over medium-high heat, heat oil. Add peppers and sauté for 4–5 minutes, until softened. Season with salt and pepper.

  Transfer grits to a bowl. Serve with the peppers.

Tip: Leftover grits can be cooled and then fried off as savory polenta-like cakes. Pour leftover grits in a shallow baking dish and refrigerate until needed. When ready to serve, cut grits into squares. Heat 2 Tbsp butter in a frying pan over medium heat, add grits in a single layer, and fry for 5 minutes, until golden. Flip and cook for another 4 minutes, until golden. Transfer to a plate and serve immediately.

Wild Rice, Roasted Mushrooms, and Italian Sausage
with Pine Nuts

Serves 4

1 cup wild rice
4 cups hot chicken stock or water
  (divided)
Salt and pepper, to taste
2 mild Italian sausage
2 Tbsp extra virgin olive oil
  (divided)
1 small white onion, finely chopped
1 cup cremini mushrooms,
  quartered
1 clove garlic, finely chopped
½ cup long-grain white rice
¼ cup pine nuts
¼ cup finely chopped parsley

Even though Canada is the number one producer of wild rice in the world, we don't cook with it enough and it's an absolute shame. This high-fiber ingredient has an irresistible nutty taste, and absorbs flavors beautifully. The combination of the sausage and the mushrooms works beautifully when combined with the sweet nuttiness of the wild rice. It's time to rethink wild rice.

Preheat the oven to 350°F.

In an ovenproof saucepan over high heat, combine wild rice and 3 cups of stock (or water) and bring to a boil. Season with salt and pepper. Cover, transfer to oven and cook for 1½ hours, until cooked through and some of the grains have burst open. (Fluff rice halfway through cooking and add more water if necessary.)

Meanwhile, in a nonstick skillet over medium heat, cook sausage for 10–12 minutes, until golden and cooked through. Remove from heat. Transfer to a plate and set aside.

In a large skillet over medium-high heat, heat 1 Tbsp oil. Add onions and mushrooms and cook for 5 minutes, until onions are softened and translucent. Add the garlic and sauté for another minute. Add remaining 1 Tbsp oil and the white rice and cook for 1 minute. Season with salt and pepper.

Transfer white rice mixture to a large baking dish with a lid. Slice the sausages and place on top of rice. Sprinkle pine nuts overtop and pour in remaining 1 cup of hot chicken stock. Cover and bake for 20–30 minutes, until rice is cooked.

Remove baking dish from oven. Add wild rice and season with salt and pepper. Mix well. Sprinkle with parsley and serve.

VARIATION:

1 Wild Rice with Roasted Mushrooms and Pine Nuts Eliminate the sausage, replace the chicken stock with vegetable stock, and add ½ cup cranberries.

Curried Rice Salad
with Currants and Cashews

This is my favorite summer salad when I have visitors over for a barbecue. Thanks to the cultural diversity in Canada, curry is more popular than ever. When introducing the spice to kids (or those unfamiliar with it), balance out the warm, earthy flavors with the sweetness of citrus and fruit.

Line a baking sheet with parchment paper.

Heat oil in a medium saucepan over high heat. Add onions and garlic, and sauté for 2 minutes. Add rice, curry powder, and ground cumin and stir for 1 minute, until rice and onions are coated in spices.

Add currants, water, and salt and bring to a boil. Stir gently and reduce heat to low. Cover and cook for 15 minutes. Remove saucepan from heat. Spread mixture on the prepared baking sheet, and chill in the refrigerator until cooled.

Transfer the rice mixture to a large bowl. Add parsley, cilantro, lemon juice, oil, and scallions and mix well. Season with salt and pepper. Sprinkle with cashews (or pistachios) for added crunch and flavor and serve.

VARIATION:

1 Curried Fruit Rice Salad Replace the currants with apricots, mangoes, cranberries, or cherries. Serve this salad warm or cold.

Serves 4

1½ Tbsp olive oil
1 small onion, finely chopped
1 clove garlic, finely chopped
2 cups basmati rice, rinsed
2 tsp curry powder
½ tsp ground cumin
½ cup dried currants
3½ cups water
1 tsp salt, plus extra to taste
¼ cup finely chopped parsley
¼ cup finely chopped cilantro
6 Tbsp lemon juice
2 tsp olive oil
2 scallions, sliced
Pepper, to taste
¼ cup toasted cashews or pistachios

Tri-Colored Quinoa
with Black Beans, Spicy Vinaigrette, and Parsley

Quinoa, like corn, comes in a variety of colors, each with a distinct taste and texture. Combining them makes for a delicious contrast of textures. Black beans are wildly underrated in Canada, and I hope this recipe will convince home cooks to appreciate them as much as I do. This is a great dish to make ahead and bring to a potluck or summer barbecue.

To make the quinoa, in a large pot over medium-high heat, bring water to a boil. Add quinoa and cook for 10–15 minutes, until soft. Remove from heat and drain. Set aside to cool.

To make the spicy vinaigrette, in a small bowl, whisk vinegar and lemon juice. Add cilantro, garlic, Sriracha, and honey. Season with salt and pepper.

In a large bowl, combine quinoa, black beans, red peppers, onions, tomato, parsley, and vinaigrette and mix well. Season with salt and pepper and serve.

VARIATION:

1 Orzo with Black Beans, Spicy Vinaigrette, and Parsley Replace the cooked quinoa with 3 cups cooked orzo pasta.

Serves 4

Quinoa
4 cups water
1 cup tri-colored quinoa, rinsed
1 (14-oz) can black beans, drained and rinsed
½ red bell pepper, seeded and cut into ¼-inch pieces
1 red onion, chopped
1 small tomato, seeded and chopped
¼ cup finely chopped parsley

Spicy vinaigrette
¼ cup red wine vinegar
2 Tbsp lemon juice
2 Tbsp cilantro, finely chopped
1 clove garlic, finely chopped
1 tsp Sriracha sauce
1 Tbsp honey
Salt and pepper, to taste

Braised Puy Lentils

Serves 4

1 Tbsp extra virgin olive oil
1 small white onion, finely chopped
1 carrot, finely chopped
1 stalk celery, finely chopped
1 clove garlic
1¼ cups Puy lentils
3½ cups vegetable stock or water
1 bay leaf
1 tsp thyme, finely chopped
Salt and pepper, to taste

When you study the French culinary tradition, some dishes never leave you. This dish is made with seemingly ordinary ingredients, but is pure kitchen magic. Lentils are a great way to get more fiber and nutrition into your diet. And bonus, this recipe is kid approved (at least in our house).

In a large saucepan over medium heat, heat oil. Add onions, carrots, celery, and garlic and cook for 10–12 minutes, until cooked through.

Add lentils, vegetable stock (or water), bay leaf, thyme, and salt and bring to a boil. Reduce heat to medium-low and simmer, covered, for 20–30 minutes, until lentils are tender and have absorbed most of the stock. Season with salt and pepper.

Transfer to a serving platter and serve immediately.

VARIATION:

1 **Braised Puy Lentils with Greens** Once the lentils are cooked and tender, add 3 cups chopped spinach, kale, or beet greens and a splash of white wine and cook for another 4 minutes.

Za'atar Israeli Couscous
with Chimichurri

Israeli (or pearl) couscous is actually a type of pasta that has the chewy texture of a grain, such as a barley. While bland on its own, Israeli couscous benefits from strong seasoning and flavors. In this instance, I've paired it with za'atar—a Middle Eastern spice blend of aromatic thyme, nutty sesame seeds, and tangy sumac—and an Argentinian sauce called chimichurri. This fresh and vibrant dish has a powerful herbaceous hit.

To make the couscous, preheat the oven to 400°F.

In a medium saucepan, combine water, salt, and za'atar and bring to a boil over high heat. Slowly add couscous and reduce heat to low. Cover and simmer for 10 minutes, or until the water is absorbed.

In a small bowl, combine squash, 1 Tbsp olive oil, and salt and pepper and mix well. Transfer to a baking sheet and roast for 12–15 minutes, until soft and slightly browned. Remove from oven and set aside.

In the same bowl, combine bell pepper, 1 Tbsp olive oil, and salt and pepper and mix well. Transfer to a baking sheet and roast for 6–8 minutes, until golden brown.

In a medium skillet over medium-high heat, melt butter. Add onions and season with salt and pepper. Cook for 10–15 minutes, stirring occasionally, until onions are softened and golden.

To make the chimichurri, in a medium bowl, combine all ingredients and mix well. Set aside.

In a large bowl, combine couscous, peppers, squash, onions, apricots, chickpeas, mint, and lemon juice and mix well. Stir in chimichurri. Season with salt and pepper and serve.

VARIATION:

1 **Baked Acorn Squash Stuffed with Spiced Couscous** Preheat the oven to 400°F. Cut 2 acorn squash in half lengthwise and brush the insides with 2 Tbsp of melted butter. Bake on a baking sheet for 20 minutes, until tender. Season with salt and pepper. Replace the chimichurri with lemon vinaigrette (page 94). Serve prepared couscous in the squash halves.

Serves 4

Za'atar couscous
1½ cups water
¼ tsp salt
1 tsp za'atar spice
1 cup Israeli couscous
1 cup butternut squash, peeled, seeded and finely chopped
2 Tbsp olive oil (divided)
Salt and pepper, to taste
1 red bell pepper, seeded and finely chopped
2 Tbsp butter
1 small white onion, finely chopped
½ cup dried apricots, sliced
½ cup chickpeas, drained and rinsed
¼ cup thinly sliced mint
2 Tbsp lemon juice

Chimichurri
¼ cup red wine vinegar
2 cloves garlic, finely chopped
1 small red onion, finely chopped
¼ cup finely chopped parsley
¼ cup finely chopped cilantro
1 Tbsp orange juice
1 tsp orange zest
¼ cup extra virgin olive oil
Salt and pepper, to taste

SUGAR AND SPICE

Homemade desserts are the ultimate expression of love. With a large family of six, we had myriad birthdays, events, and celebratory occasions around the year. And no matter how busy she was, my mother always committed to making homemade treats for these moments. The ingredients and stand mixer would be sprawled across the flour-dusted farmhouse table, where the children congregated and battled it out to determine who would get to lick the spatula. The gorgeous warm and spiced scent of freshly baked hot cross buns or cinnamon rolls frequently wafted through our home.

Over the years, she produced some iconic desserts. Her communal dessert—Carole's Famous Carrot Cake with Cream Cheese and Candied Orange Frosting page 170—would show up at potlucks and baby showers (and happened to be an easy way for us to get in our vegetables). Just-Like-Mom's Pudding page 173 was the highlight of weekday suppers. She showed me that an unassuming pound cake or meringue can easily dress up as a showstopper that can make your friends and family feel valued and special.

So I've come up with some favorites. With three boys who inherited my sweet tooth, we stick to simpler desserts such as Cookie Whoopie Pie page 169. I've found out over the years that adults enjoy this treat as much as children. For more grown-up gatherings, Ginger Crème Brûlée page 183 is my nod to a classic. Salted-Caramel Bundt Cake page 176 makes a winning finale to any meal, and a dramatic Strawberry Tarte Tatin page 175 is heaven on earth. One can fall in love with a dessert before tasting it.

Cookie Whoopie Pie

Serves 4

½ cup (1 stick) butter, softened
1 cup packed brown sugar
1 egg
1 tsp vanilla extract
1 cup all-purpose flour
½ tsp baking powder
½ tsp baking soda
Pinch of salt
1¼ cups rolled oats
¾ cup chocolate chips
¾ cup chopped pecans
2 cups vanilla ice cream
¾ cup Oreo cookie crumbs

Traditionally, whoopie pies are made by sandwiching a meringue-style frosting between two soft, cake-like cookies. My version is more like an ice-cream sandwich made with highly addictive cookies. This may be an unconventional dinner party dish, but trust me, nothing lights up people's eyes quite like cookie sandwiches.

Preheat the oven to 350°F. Line a baking sheet with parchment paper.

In the bowl of a stand mixer fitted with the paddle attachment, combine butter and brown sugar and beat until light and fluffy. Add egg and vanilla and beat until smooth.

In a medium bowl, combine flour, baking powder, baking soda, and salt and mix well. Add dry ingredients to the butter mixture and beat until just combined. Add rolled oats, chocolate chips, and pecans and beat until just combined.

Scoop 8 large balls of cookie dough onto the prepared baking sheet, 2 inches apart. Using a fork, gently flatten the cookie dough to a ½-inch thickness. Bake for 12–15 minutes, until golden. Remove from oven and set aside to cool completely.

To serve, scoop ½ cup ice cream onto the flat side of four cookies. Top with another cookie and roll each sandwich in the cookie crumbs.

VARIATIONS:

1 Cookie Whoopie Pie with Toffee and Dried Cherries Replace the nuts with dried cherries and replace the chocolate chips with crumbled toffee.

2 Cookie Whoopie Pie with Cream Cheese and Orange Replace the ice cream with 1 cup whipped cream cheese mixed with 1 Tbsp icing sugar and zest from half an orange.

Carole's Famous Carrot Cake
with Cream Cheese and Candied Orange Frosting

Serves 4

Carrot cake
¾ cup packed brown sugar
2 Tbsp butter, softened, plus extra
 for greasing
¼ cup vegetable oil
2 eggs
¾ cup all-purpose flour
¾ tsp baking powder
½ tsp baking soda
½ tsp ground cinnamon
¼ tsp ground ginger
1¼ cups grated carrot
¼ cup walnuts, coarsely chopped
¼ cup pecans, coarsely chopped
¼ cup raisins

Frosting
1 cup cream cheese, softened
¾ cup icing sugar
½ vanilla bean
1 Tbsp candied orange zest

I remember there always being tons of carrots around when growing up on the farm. They were often made into classic dishes, like soups and casseroles, or even mashed or candied. But it was my mother's carrot cake that always topped the list for us kids. With the sweetness of raisins, the texture of crunchy walnuts and pecans, and creamy, tangy frosting, this seemingly retro dessert is anything but old-fashioned.

To make the cake, preheat the oven to 350°F. Grease 4 (8-oz) ramekins and set aside.

In the bowl of a stand mixer fitted with the paddle attachment, combine brown sugar, 2 Tbsp butter, and oil and beat until smooth, occasionally scraping down sides of the bowl. Add eggs, one at a time, mixing after each addition. Mix for another minute, or until just combined.

In a medium bowl, combine flour, baking powder, baking soda, cinnamon, and ginger and mix well. Add to the butter mixture, along with carrots, nuts, and raisins. Mix until just combined.

Divide batter among the prepared ramekins and bake for 20 minutes, or until a toothpick inserted into the center comes out clean. Set aside to cool.

Meanwhile, make the frosting. In a large bowl, beat cream cheese until creamy. Slowly add icing sugar, then scrape in the seeds from the vanilla pod.

To serve, top each cake with a dollop of cream cheese icing and garnish with candied orange zest.

VARIATION:

1 Chocolate Zucchini Cake Replace the grated carrots with 1 cup grated zucchini and replace the raisins with chocolate chips.

Banana and Dark Chocolate Bread Pudding *with Crème Anglaise*

Made with simple ingredients, the humble bread pudding feeds you on a deep level. This basic recipe is elevated with classic childhood flavors—chocolate and bananas—making it the ultimate comfort dish that's perfect for sharing on a cold winter's night.

To make the bread pudding, preheat the oven to 350°F. Grease 4 (8-oz) ramekins (or an 8 × 8-inch baking dish) and set aside. Line a baking sheet with parchment paper.

Spread bread cubes on the prepared baking sheet and toast for 5–7 minutes, until golden brown and dry. Remove from oven and set aside.

Meanwhile, in a large bowl, combine eggs, egg yolks, half-and-half, whipping cream, brown sugar, vanilla, and cinnamon and mix well.

Divide the bread cubes, banana slices, and chocolate evenly among the greased ramekins. Pour egg mixture into each ramekin and bake for 30–35 minutes, until set. (Or 45 minutes in a baking dish.) Remove from oven and set aside to cool until serving.

To make the crème anglaise, in a small saucepan over medium-high heat, combine whipping cream and 1 tsp vanilla and bring to a gentle boil. Remove from heat as soon as it comes to a boil and set aside.

In a small bowl, combine egg yolks and sugar and whisk. While whisking continuously, slowly add half of the hot cream. Still whisking, gradually pour the egg mixture back into the saucepan of cream. Turn heat to low and cook for 5 minutes, stirring continuously, until the mixture coats the back of a wooden spoon. (Do not let it boil.)

Serve bread pudding with the warm crème anglaise.

VARIATIONS:

1 **Peaches and Cream Bread Pudding** Replace the banana and chopped chocolate with 1 cup drained and chopped canned peaches and ¾ cup firm cream cheese, cut into small pieces. Bake as instructed.

2 **Grandma Mollison's Original Cinnamon and Raisin Bread Pudding** Instead of dicing the bread, slice it. Replace the banana and chocolate with 1 cup rum-soaked raisins. Place the bread pudding in a large baking dish and bake for 25–30 minutes.

Serves 4

Bread pudding
Butter, for greasing
¾ lb loaf brioche or challah (including end pieces), cut into 1-inch cubes
3 eggs
2 egg yolks
1 cup half-and-half (10%) cream
1 cup whipping (35%) cream
1 cup packed brown sugar
1 tsp vanilla extract
1½ tsp ground cinnamon
2 bananas, cut into ¼-inch-thick slices
½ cup dark bitter chocolate, coarsely chopped

Crème anglaise
1 cup whipping (35%) cream
1 tsp vanilla extract
4 egg yolks
6 Tbsp granulated sugar

Tip: If you're pressed for time, simply serve the bread pudding with your favorite ice cream or vanilla whipped cream.

Just-Like-Mom's Pudding

Pudding is a catch-all term for a lot of desserts, from British posset to French *pots de crème,* but this is a classic version steeped in tradition. When the air turns brisk and you're craving something warming, this pudding—amped up with a hint of whiskey—is quintessential comfort in a bowl. Best of all, if you're planning to serve it at a party, it can be prepared up to three days in advance.

To make the pudding, in a double boiler over medium-high heat, heat milk for 5 minutes, until scalded. Stir in whiskey (or brandy) and set aside.

In a medium bowl, combine flour, cocoa, sugar, and salt and mix well. Pour in 1 cup scalded milk, stirring vigorously until well combined and smooth. Add mixture back to the double boiler and stir vigorously. Cook for 15 minutes over medium-high heat, until mixture coats the back of a spoon.

Crack eggs into a medium bowl and beat. Add a small amount of chocolate mixture to the eggs and stir continuously to temper (this prevents the eggs from scrambling when added to the hot mixture). Pour tempered egg mixture into double boiler and cook for 3–5 minutes, until thickened. Remove from heat. Stir in 1 tsp vanilla and then refrigerate until cooled completely, about 4 hours.

To make the whipped cream, in the bowl of a stand mixer fitted with the whisk attachment, whip cream until soft peaks form. Add sugar and vanilla and gently mix.

To serve, spoon pudding into bowls and top with a dollop of whipped cream and raspberries.

Serves 4

Pudding
4 cups milk
3 Tbsp whiskey or brandy
½ cup all-purpose flour
6 Tbsp cocoa
1½ cups granulated sugar
Pinch of salt
2 eggs
1 tsp vanilla extract
1 cup raspberries, to serve

Whipped cream
1 cup whipping (35%) cream
1 Tbsp granulated sugar
½ tsp vanilla extract

Tip: Use the pudding as a custard-like filling in any home-baked cake to add a layer of creaminess.

Strawberry Tarte Tatin

Serves 4

3–4 cups strawberries, washed, hulled, and uniform in size
¼ cup granulated sugar
2 Tbsp water
2 Tbsp butter
1 large sheet puff pastry, thawed and cut into a 10-inch round
1 egg, beaten
¼ cup crème fraîche or sour cream, to serve
Mint leaves, to garnish

Tarte tatin is an ingenious French dessert packed with a contrast of flavors and textures and is deceptively easy to prepare. Traditionally, tarte tatin is made with apples, but this strawberry version captures the essence of summer. To maximize flavor, I strongly recommend using fresh strawberries or other seasonal fruits (see variations below for options).

Preheat the oven to 425°F.

Trim tops of strawberries to form flat surfaces.

In an 8-inch cast-iron skillet over medium heat, combine sugar and water and cook for 7–10 minutes, swirling the skillet until sugar turns golden brown (avoid stirring). Add butter and swirl the skillet, until butter is melted and incorporated. Remove from heat and set aside to cool for 2–3 minutes.

Carefully place strawberries, flat-side down, into the skillet, arranging in concentric circles starting along the outside edge. (Make sure they fit snugly together.) Lay puff pastry sheet over strawberries, tucking excess pastry around the inside edge of the skillet. Brush puff pastry with egg. Bake for 15–20 minutes, until puff pastry has puffed up and is golden brown.

Remove tarte from oven and set aside to rest for 5 minutes. Carefully invert onto a large plate or serving platter. Cut into slices and serve with a dollop of crème fraîche (or sour cream).

VARIATIONS:

1 Stone-Fruit Tarte Tatin Replace the strawberries with 5 halved and pitted peaches or 10 apricots or 4 cups whole pitted cherries.

2 Banana Tarte Tatin Replace the strawberries with 4–5 unripe bananas, cut into 1½-inch-thick slices.

3 Apple or Pear Tarte Tatin Replace the strawberries with 6 peeled and sliced apples (preferably Granny Smith) or pears (any kind).

Salted-Caramel Bundt Cake

We often had Bundt cakes at our house in case company dropped in: my mother would brew fresh coffee, slice up the ready-made cake, and everyone would gather in the kitchen to chat. Named after the ring pan in which they're made, Bundt cakes draw inspiration from a popular Austrian dessert called *kugelhopf*. This classic dessert makes a striking showpiece at dinner parties and requires absolutely no fuss.

To make the cake, preheat the oven to 350°F. Grease a 7½ × 3-inch Bundt pan.

In the bowl of a stand mixer fitted with the paddle attachment, combine flour, sugar, baking powder, and salt and mix well. Add butter and beat until combined. Add eggs, one at a time, beating until combined after each addition. Add buttermilk and vanilla and beat for another 3 minutes.

Pour batter into the prepared Bundt pan and bake for 30–40 minutes, or until a toothpick inserted into the center comes out clean. Set aside.

Meanwhile, make the caramel-butter sauce. In a small saucepan over medium-low heat, combine caramels, hot water, and butter and stir until melted. (Do not allow it to boil.)

While the cake is still warm, prick holes on the top of the cake and pour caramel-butter sauce overtop. Set aside to cool for 15–20 minutes, and then invert the cake onto a serving plate. Set aside to cool completely.

Meanwhile, make the salted-caramel sauce. In a medium saucepan over medium-low heat, combine caramels and whipping cream and stir until melted. Stir in vanilla and butter until smooth. Stir in salt, remove from heat and set aside.

To serve, drizzle salted-caramel sauce over the Bundt cake and slice.

VARIATIONS:

1 **Apple and Cinnamon Bundt Cake** Add 1 cup cooked apples, ¾ cup chopped walnuts, and 1 tsp cinnamon to the cake batter after it is in the pan.

2 **Raspberries and Cream Bundt Cake** Add 1½ cups raspberries and 5 Tbsp cream cheese to the cake batter after it is in the pan.

Serves 4

Cake
½ cup (1 stick) butter, softened, plus extra for greasing
1½ cups all-purpose flour
1 cup granulated sugar
½ tsp baking powder
Pinch of salt
2 eggs
1 cup buttermilk
1 tsp vanilla extract

Caramel-butter sauce
½ cup store-bought caramels
2 Tbsp hot water
3 Tbsp butter

Salted-caramel sauce
1 cup store-bought caramels
5 Tbsp whipping (35%) cream
1 tsp vanilla extract
2 Tbsp butter, softened
½ tsp salt

Stone-Fruit Crumble

Crumble is a simple and irresistible dish that bakes beautifully, especially when it's made with stone fruit. And the oaty texture, toasted sweetness, and vanilla ice cream in this recipe bring out the best in the stone fruit while letting its flavor shine through. It also travels well and can be reheated in the oven in the time that it takes you to eat your dinner.

To make the filling, preheat the oven to 350°F. Lightly grease an 8-inch baking dish.

In a medium bowl, combine fruit, brown sugar, tapioca starch, cinnamon, lemon juice, and salt and mix well. Pour into the prepared baking dish and set aside.

To make the crumble, in a small bowl, combine brown sugar, butter, flour, and salt. Using your fingertips, mix until a coarse crumble forms. Add oats and gently mix, until just combined. Sprinkle mixture over filling, coating fruit evenly.

Bake for 25–30 minutes, until golden and bubbling. Set aside to cool for 5 minutes.

To serve, scoop crumble into 4 bowls and top each with ice cream.

VARIATIONS:

1 Orchard Fruit Crumble Replace the stone fruit with 1½ cups chopped apples and 1½ cups chopped pears.

2 Strawberry and Rhubarb Crumble Replace the stone fruit with 3 cups chopped strawberries and 1 cup chopped rhubarb.

3 Pear and Cranberry Crumble Replace the stone fruit with 3 cups chopped pear and ⅔ cup fresh cranberries.

Serves 4–6

Filling
Butter, for greasing
2 peaches, pitted and sliced
4 plums, pitted and sliced
2 nectarines, pitted and sliced
3 Tbsp firmly packed brown sugar
1½ Tbsp tapioca starch
½ tsp ground cinnamon
1 tsp lemon juice
Pinch of salt
Vanilla ice cream, to serve

Crumble
¼ cup firmly packed brown sugar
¼ cup (½ stick) butter, softened
¼ cup all-purpose flour
Pinch of salt
¼ cup quick oats

Chocolate Cake
with Pecan-Caramel Sauce

Chocolate cake is one of life's most indulgent pleasures: it warms the heart and feeds the soul. This recipe is rich, moist, and topped with a luxurious pecan-caramel sauce, making it a thoroughly grown-up treat for special occasions.

To make the cake, preheat the oven to 350°F. Grease a 9 × 5-inch loaf pan.

In the bowl of a stand mixer fitted with the paddle attachment, combine butter, sugar, eggs, milk, and vanilla and beat until combined.

In a small bowl, sift together flour, cocoa, baking powder, and salt. Slowly add dry ingredients to egg mixture and beat until just combined.

Pour batter into the prepared loaf pan and bake for 30 minutes, or until a toothpick inserted into the center comes out clean. Remove from oven and set aside to cool.

To make the pecan-caramel sauce, in a medium saucepan over medium-low heat, combine caramels and water and stir until smooth and creamy. Stir in pecans and set aside.

To serve, slice cake and serve on individual plates, topped with ice cream, raspberries, and a drizzle of warm pecan-caramel sauce.

VARIATION:

1 Banana and Coconut Cake Add ¾ cup mashed banana and ½ cup unsweetened shredded coconut to the batter.

Serves 4

Cake
6 Tbsp butter, melted, plus extra
  for greasing
½ cup granulated sugar
2 eggs
2 Tbsp milk
¾ tsp vanilla extract
6 Tbsp all-purpose flour
¼ cup cocoa
½ tsp baking powder
Pinch of salt
Vanilla ice cream, to serve
1 cup raspberries, to serve

Pecan-caramel sauce
½ (14-oz) package caramels
¼ cup hot water
½ cup chopped pecans, toasted

Spiced Chocolate Molten Cake

Serves 4

1¼ cups (2½ sticks) butter, plus
    extra for greasing
¾ cup chopped dark chocolate
2 eggs
2 egg yolks
3 Tbsp icing sugar
2 tsp all-purpose flour, plus extra
    for dusting
¼ tsp ground cinnamon
Pinch of ground ginger
Pinch of ground nutmeg
Pinch of salt
Raspberries, to garnish
Whipped cream or your favorite
    ice cream, to serve (optional)

Consider this molten chocolate cake for formal dinners when you want to present a restaurant-style dessert. It's easy to prep, has great presentation, and is just enough to elegantly cap off a meal.

Preheat the oven to 425°F. Grease and flour 4 (8-oz) ramekins and set aside.

In a medium saucepan over medium heat, combine butter and chocolate and heat until melted and smooth. Remove from heat and set aside for 15 minutes to cool.

In the bowl of a stand mixer fitted with the whisk attachment, combine eggs, egg yolks, and icing sugar and whisk until mixture is pale and thick. Continuing to whisk, slowly pour in chocolate mixture and whisk for 1–2 minutes, until incorporated and mixed through.

In a small bowl, combine flour, cinnamon, ginger, nutmeg, and salt and mix well. Using a spatula, fold dry ingredients into the chocolate mixture. Divide batter among the prepared ramekins and set on a baking sheet. Bake for 8–10 minutes, until set.

Invert the ramekins onto serving plates and serve immediately with raspberries and whipped cream or your favorite ice cream, if using.

VARIATIONS:

1 Holiday Peppermint Chocolate Cakes Add 2 Tbsp crushed peppermint candies or candy cane to the batter. Dust the baked molten cakes with icing sugar or cocoa powder and serve with fresh mixed berries.

2 Chocolate Hazelnut Molten Cake Add 2 Tbsp chocolate liqueur with eggs and add 1 Tbsp ground hazelnuts with dry ingredients.

Ginger Crème Brûlée

While the addition of ginger makes this a less-than-traditional take on classic crème brûlée, the end result remains just as silky, light, and elegant with the right balance of warmth and spice. It's deceptively easy to make and can be prepared ahead of time for parties—simply brûlée right before serving.

Serves 4

1 cup half-and-half (10%) cream
1 cup whipping (35%) cream
6 thin slices ginger, peeled
6 egg yolks
⅓ cup + 2 Tbsp granulated sugar
    (divided)
1½ tsp vanilla extract
Pinch of salt
Fresh gooseberries and currants,
    to garnish (optional)

Preheat the oven to 325°F.

In a large saucepan over medium high heat, combine half-and-half, whipping cream, and ginger. Heat until it just starts to boil. Remove from heat. Using a fine-mesh sieve, strain into a bowl.

In a medium bowl, combine egg yolks, ¾ cup sugar, vanilla, and salt and mix well. Slowly add a third of the hot cream to egg mixture, stirring vigorously to temper (this prevents the eggs from scrambling when added to the hot mixture). Add the mixture to the saucepan of cream, stirring vigorously. Strain the mixture through a fine-mesh sieve.

Place 4 ovenproof jars into a shallow baking dish. Pour mixture into the jars. Fill the shallow baking dish halfway with hot water. Cover baking dish with foil and bake for 30 minutes, or until crème brûlée is just set. Chill in the refrigerator for at least 2 hours.

Remove crème brûlée from the refrigerator at least 30 minutes before serving. Sprinkle each brûlée with remaining 2 Tbsp sugar. Using a kitchen torch, melt the sugar until it is crisp and amber in color. Garnish with gooseberries and currants, if using. Serve.

VARIATIONS:

1 Traditional Crème Brûlée Eliminate the ginger.

2 Chocolate Crème Brûlée Replace the ginger with 3 Tbsp cocoa powder added to the warm custard.

3 Orange Crème Brûlée Replace the ginger with 1 orange, cut into ½-inch slices. Strain.

SOMETHING
TO
SIP

A good drinks menu sets the mood, enhances the ingredients in your dishes, and adds to the festivity. It's tempting to stock a party with just wine and beer, but with a little know-how and minimal effort you can create professional-level cocktails that will enhance the convivial spirit. I like to explore my options by working with seasonal fruits, vegetables, and herbs—Sangria page 193 is the perfect example.

When creating a drink, think about the base (produce) and then build with spirits. A Pimm's Pitcher page 190 is a quintessential summer quencher for barbecues and al fresco gatherings, while Winter Mulled Wine page 189 truly captures the mood of winter festivities. And sometimes it's easier to let guests serve themselves with the help of a Bloody Mary and Caesar Bar page 188.

Not all occasions call for alcohol. At a children's party or an afternoon picnic, consider a refreshing Cucumber and Basil Lemonade page 187. When we've spent long afternoons at the hockey rink or on the slopes, we treat ourselves to Chai Hot Chocolate with Chocolate-Banana Pillows page 195. I can't think of a better way to finish a day.

Cucumber and Basil Lemonade

Serves 4

1 cup granulated sugar
1½ cups lemon juice
1 lemon, thinly sliced, plus extra
    to garnish
7 cups cold water
2 cups sliced English cucumber
½ cup basil leaves, plus extra to
    garnish

When the mercury rises and the heat is on, no drink says summer quite like lemonade. This humble beverage gets a modern makeover with cucumber and basil—your kids' lemonade stand will never be the same.

In a large glass pitcher, combine sugar and lemon juice. Stir to mix until sugar is completely dissolved. Add lemon slices and water, then cucumbers and basil.

Refrigerate for 4 hours.

Fill 4 tall glasses with ice and pour lemonade overtop. Garnish each glass with a lemon slice and basil leaves and serve with a tall straw.

VARIATIONS:

1 Summer Chiller Fill a blender halfway with ice. Add lemonade and a splash of vodka, gin, or bourbon. Purée the mixture until slushy and serve.

2 Rosemary Berry Fizz Replace the cucumbers with 2 cups sliced strawberries. Reduce the water to 5 cups. Add 2 cans club soda. Replace the basil with rosemary.

3 Watermelon and Raspberry Lemonade In a blender or food processor, purée 3 cups chopped watermelon. Fill an ice cube tray with mixture and freeze overnight. Prepare the lemonade as instructed above, eliminating the cucumber and basil and adding 1½ cups raspberries. Fill 4 glasses with frozen watermelon cubes and pour the lemonade overtop. Garnish each tall glass with a lemon slice and a small sprig of mint. (You could also add 1½ oz of gin or tequila to each glass.)

Bloody Mary and Caesar Bar

When putting a bar together for a party, consider preparing a signature drink—not only will it give you a better sense of your guests' consumption, but it can be more economical as well. The Caesar is the Canadian version of the Blood Mary and is, arguably, improved with Clamato. Simply prepare a fun combination of assorted bases, spirits, seasonings, aromatics, and garnishes and let your guests customize their own drinks.

Base (3 parts)
Tomato juice
Clamato juice
Tomato- and vegetable-blend juice

Spirit (1 part)
Vodka
Gin
Beer
Rum
Tequila
Whiskey

Seasoning
Celery salt
Chili powder
Hot sauces
Horseradish
Citrus juice
Soy sauce
Worcestershire sauce
Olive brine
Pickle brine
Hoisin sauce
BBQ sauce

Garnish
Lemon or lime wedges
Olives
Pickles such as cucumbers, beets, hot peppers, asparagus, beans, carrots, or pearl onions
Celery stalks
Long carrot sticks
Fennel and anise spears
Baby peppers
Chicken Wings (page 44)
Whole poached shrimp
Pepperettes
Candied bacon
Fresh shucked oysters
BBQ pork

Rim
Celery salt
Salt and pepper (in equal parts)
Jalapeno salt
Smoked salt
Crumbled bacon
Lime juice and salt

Winter Mulled Wine

Serves 4

*1 bottle red wine such as Merlot
   or Beaujolais
¼ cup brandy
¼ cup granulated sugar
3 whole cloves
3 cardamom pods
1 small cinnamon stick
1 star anise
1 small sprig rosemary
1 small orange, sliced, to serve*

Mulled wine is a spiced, fortified wine drink that helps people forget about the winter cold. This easy-to-make version can be prepared ahead of time in a slow cooker, meaning you can set it up, go tobogganing, and come back to a delicious warm-up. Don't skip the orange garnish—its subtle tang complements the deeply spiced flavors.

In a slow cooker, combine all ingredients except orange slices and stir to mix until sugar is completely dissolved. Cover and heat on low for 30–45 minutes, until warm.

   Divide sliced orange among 4 large mugs. Carefully ladle mulled wine into the mugs and serve.

VARIATIONS:

1 Non-Alcoholic Mulled "Wine" Replace the red wine with pomegranate juice.

2 Orchard Cider Replace the red wine with 2 cups of apple juice and 1 cup of cranberry juice. Replace the cardamom with a small piece of peeled ginger. Replace the rosemary with 1 orange, sliced into ½-inch rounds.

Pimm's Pitcher

Serves 4

²⁄₃ cup mint leaves
½ lemon, cut into small wedges
4 cups ice
1 orange, peeled and segmented
⅓ English cucumber, thinly sliced
1 cup strawberries, quartered
1½ cups Pimm's No. 1
1 cup lemonade
1 cup ginger ale or club soda

When Anthea Turner and I filmed *Dinner Party Wars* during the heat of the summer, we drank these by the gallon. This flavored gin cocktail—infused with cucumber, mint, and strawberries—may sound like the makings of a summer salad, but in actuality, it's a quintessential summer cocktail that's been served in Britain for centuries. Pimm's is a type of liqueur with a distinct flavor: slightly bitter with a hint of orange and herbal notes that carry fresh ingredients with ease.

In a large clear glass pitcher, combine mint and lemons. Using a wooden spoon, muddle.

Pour ice into the pitcher and then add remaining ingredients. Stir and serve.

VARIATIONS:

1 Lychee and Raspberry Pimm's Replace the strawberries with ½ cup fresh or frozen raspberries and ½ cup canned lychee fruit, chopped.

2 Watermelon Moscow Mule Replace the oranges, cucumber, and strawberries with 4 cups of chopped watermelon and 1 can of ginger beer. Replace the Pimm's with vodka.

Balsamic and Peppered Strawberry Champagne Charger

Serves 4

½ cup chopped strawberries
2 oz vodka
1 Tbsp simple sugar syrup
½ tsp balsamic vinegar
1 basil leaf
Coarsely ground black pepper,
    to taste
2 cups champagne or sparkling
    wine

Nothing speaks of Toronto more than the weekly tradition of brunch: people will line up for over an hour to eat at their favorite restaurant or diner. As drinks are a big part of the appeal, this easy but elegant drink is designed for days of leisure.

In a small cocktail shaker, combine strawberries, vodka, syrup, vinegar, basil, and pepper and shake until strawberries are puréed. Using a bar/cocktail strainer, pour into 4 champagne flutes.

   Pour champagne (or sparkling wine) into each flute and serve.

VARIATIONS:

1 **Strawberry Mimosas** Eliminate the vodka and prepare as instructed.

2 **Raspberry and Mint Champagne Charger** Replace the basil with mint and the strawberries with raspberries.

Sangria

Sangria is so popular these days and comes in many varieties—made with white, rosé, sparkling, and red wine—at bars. If you don't want to put out the typical punch for a holiday party, the White Wine Sangria is a fantastic option. This is a very fruity version of Sangria that's almost pie-like with the addition of the cinnamon, cloves, and sage. It sounds a little strange, but this is a crowd pleaser.

To make the red wine sangria, in a large glass pitcher, combine mango, lemon (or lime), apricots, apples, and mint, if using. Pour in red wine, schnapps, brandy, and lemonade and stir. Refrigerate for 4 hours.

To serve, pour in club soda, stir, and serve in oversized wine glasses.

To make the white wine sangria, in a large glass pitcher, combine apples, pear, cranberries, blackberries, orange slices, cinnamon, cloves, and sage. Pour in white wine, apple juice, and cranberry juice and stir. Refrigerate for 4 hours.

To serve, pour in club soda, stir, and serve in oversized wine glasses.

VARIATIONS:

1 **Summer Beer Sangria** Replace the white wine with 3 cups light beer or cider and 1 cup pineapple juice and add sliced grapefruit, oranges, and limes.

2 **Christmas Party White Sangria** Replace the apple and cranberry juice with orange and pomegranate juice and the sage with rosemary sprigs.

Serves 4

Red wine sangria
1 mango, peeled and chopped
1 lemon or lime, thinly sliced
1 cup chopped apricots
1 small apple, thinly sliced
2 large sprigs mint (optional)
1 (750-ml) bottle red wine such as Merlot
¼ cup peach schnapps
¼ cup apricot brandy
1½ cups lemonade, chilled
1 (12-fl-oz) can club soda, chilled

White wine sangria
1 small Granny Smith apple, cored and chopped
1 small pear, cored and chopped
½ cup whole cranberries
1 cup blackberries
1 orange, thinly sliced
1 small cinnamon stick
4 cloves
6 sage leaves
1 (750-ml) bottle white wine such as Sauvignon Blanc, chilled
1 cup apple juice
1 cup cranberry juice
1 (12-fl-oz) can club soda, chilled

Chai Hot Chocolate
with Chocolate-Banana Pillows

Serves 4

Chocolate-banana pillows
1 cup dark bitter chocolate
1 small banana, cut into coins

Chai hot chocolate
4 cups milk
3 Tbsp brown sugar
1 Tbsp grated ginger
4 cloves
1 large cinnamon stick, broken in half
2 star anise
4 whole cardamom pods
½ cup cocoa powder

Chai and chocolate is a sublime combination, but the addition of the chocolate banana "pillows" takes this après-ski drink to another level. (And if you're really cold, you can add some booze such as Irish Cream.) This drink should be prepared a day in advance.

To make the chocolate-banana pillows, in a small heatproof bowl set over a saucepan of simmering water over medium heat, melt chocolate. Spoon chocolate into an ice cube tray and insert banana coins into each compartment. Cover with plastic wrap and freeze overnight.

To make the chai hot chocolate, in a small saucepan over medium heat, combine all ingredients and heat for 4 minutes, until warmed through. Stir often to prevent milk from scorching. Remove from the heat and set aside to cool to room temperature. Pour the mixture into a glass container. Cover with plastic wrap and refrigerate overnight.

Using a fine-mesh sieve, strain chai mixture into a small saucepan and gently reheat over medium heat.

Fill 4 mugs with chai hot chocolate and drop a couple of frozen chocolate-banana pillows into each mug. Serve with spoons so guests can stir pillows and allow them to melt in the hot chocolate.

VARIATIONS:

1 Spiced Hot Chocolate with Mini Marshmallows and Chocolate Shavings Eliminate the cloves, ginger, and cardamom and add a pinch of cayenne. Replace chocolate-banana pillows with 1 cup mini marshmallows and ½ cup shaved chocolate.

2 Festive Chai Hot Chocolate Serve each cup with a large peppermint candy cane.

BASIC RECIPES

CORBIN'S ESSENTIAL BBQ RUB AND SPICE BLEND

2 Tbsp paprika
1 Tbsp ground cumin, toasted
1 Tbsp salt
1 Tbsp onion powder
1 Tbsp garlic powder
1½ tsp dried thyme leaves
1½ tsp ground black pepper
1½ tsp dried oregano leaves
1 tsp cayenne pepper
1 tsp white pepper

Combine all ingredients in a small resealable jar. Cover and shake well. Store in a dark cool space until use.

Tip: Add 2 tsp brown sugar to the original recipe and use as the perfect dry rub on pork ribs or chicken wings.

ROASTED GARLIC

1 head garlic
1 Tbsp olive oil

Preheat the oven to 360°F. Cut top off garlic, rub oil over garlic, and wrap in foil. Place in the oven and roast for 30 minutes, until softened and caramelized.

AIOLI

2 cloves garlic, finely chopped
2 egg yolks
Salt and pepper, to taste
1½ cups olive oil
1 tsp Dijon mustard
1 Tbsp lemon juice

In a food processer, combine garlic, egg yolks, and salt and pepper. Process until smooth. With processor running, slowly pour in oil. Process until mixture thickens to the consistency of mayonnaise.

   Transfer mixture to a small bowl and stir in mustard and lemon juice. Refrigerate and store until needed (will keep up to 4 days refrigerated).

TRUFFLE HONEY

1 cup liquid honey
1 Tbsp truffle oil

In a small bowl, combine all ingredients and mix well.

CARAMELIZED ONIONS

3 Tbsp butter
3 Tbsp olive oil
3 large yellow onions, thinly sliced

In a heavy-bottomed skillet over medium-high heat, heat butter and oil. Add onions and sauté for 10 minutes, until softened and translucent. Reduce the heat to low and cook for another 20 minutes, or until the onions are brown and caramelized. Remove from heat.

CRISPY LEEKS

3 cups vegetable oil
1 leek, white- and light-green parts only, trimmed, washed, and cut into ⅛-inch-thick slices
Salt, to taste

In a large saucepan over medium-high heat, heat oil until it reaches a temperature of 360°F. Using a paper towel, pat leeks dry. Using a slotted spoon, carefully lower into the saucepan. Deep-fry for 3–5 minutes, until golden and crispy. Using the same slotted spoon, transfer leeks to a plate lined with paper towels.

SAUTÉED BRUSSELS SPROUTS

½ Tbsp butter
1½ cups thinly sliced Brussels sprouts
Salt and pepper, to taste

In a large skillet over medium-high heat, melt butter. Add Brussels sprouts and sauté for 3–5 minutes, until Brussels sprouts are golden. Season with salt and pepper and serve.

ROASTED PLUM TOMATOES

6 ripe plum tomatoes, halved lengthwise
3 cloves garlic, finely chopped
2 Tbsp olive oil
½ tsp dried basil
½ tsp dried oregano
Salt and pepper, to taste

Preheat the oven to 300°F. Place a wire rack on a large baking sheet.

In a medium bowl, combine all ingredients and toss to mix. Place tomatoes, flesh side up, on the wire rack and roast for 45–60 minutes, until edges of tomatoes are brown. Remove from the oven and serve.

SAUTÉED MUSHROOMS

2½ Tbsp olive oil
2 cups button or field mushrooms, thinly sliced
2 cups cremini mushrooms, thinly sliced
2 cloves garlic, finely chopped
Salt and pepper, to taste

In a large skillet over medium-high heat, heat oil. Add mushrooms and garlic and sauté 8–10 minutes, until golden and cooked through. Season with salt and pepper and serve.

Tip: Replace half of the cremini or field mushrooms with wild mushrooms like oyster, chanterelle, or shiitake.

BRANDADE

½ lb boneless and skinless salt cod, soaked overnight in water
2 cloves garlic
1 large bay leaf
3 cups milk
1 cup mashed potatoes
1 Tbsp chopped dill
¼ cup whipping (35%) cream
Coarsely ground black pepper, to taste

Preheat the oven to 375°F.

Thoroughly rinse salt cod, until the water runs clear. In a shallow baking dish, combine salt cod, garlic, bay leaf, and milk. Cover with foil. Place in oven and bake for 10 minutes. Remove from the oven and set aside to cool to room temperature.

Remove cod from poaching liquid. In a food processor, combine cod, mashed potatoes, dill, and cream and purée until a smooth paste forms. Season with pepper and serve.

PIE CRUST DOUGH

1¾ cups all-purpose flour, plus extra for dusting
¾ cup (1½ sticks) butter
Pinch of salt
4–6 Tbsp cold water

To make the dough, in a food processor, combine flour, butter, and a pinch of salt. Pulse. Add a few Tbsp of water at a time and continue to pulse until a smooth dough forms. Wrap the dough in plastic wrap and let rest in the refrigerator for 30 minutes.

CANDIED BACON

¼ cup pure maple syrup
2 Tbsp brown sugar
¼ tsp red pepper flakes
½ lb sliced bacon

Preheat the oven to 375°F. Line a baking sheet with parchment paper.

In a small bowl, combine maple syrup, brown sugar, and red pepper flakes and mix well. Dip bacon slices into mixture and shake off excess. Place bacon onto prepared baking sheet and bake for 20 minutes, or until bacon is crisp and caramelized. Remove from oven and set aside to cool completely.

Chop bacon into small pieces and serve.

ACKNOWLEDGEMENTS

I started cooking professionally at 17. Thirty years later, I continue do what I love every day both at home and at work. So many people have influenced my career, and I wouldn't be here today without their support.

Thank you to my mother, grandmothers, and sister for sharing your kitchens with me. You taught me that great food brings people together and creates the most memorable stories.

I'd also like to thank all the militant executive chefs I trained under. Your leadership, dedication, and sheer discipline provided me a foundation in cooking. You taught me that hard work does pay off and that one should never give up, even at life's most challenging moments.

To my family and friends: you are my greatest fans and advocates. I have been surrounded by supportive friends, customers, clients, employers, vendors, and purveyors who have helped shape my career. I am humbled by your continuous support.

Karen Geier: you are a committed writer who has helped me express my greatest and most cherished experiences. Thank you for everything.

I'd like to extend my sincere gratitude to the creative team: Emilie for assisting with recipes and Christian, Jess, Natalie, Noah, Jenny, Laura, Maria, Analia, and Janae for bringing each and every photograph to life.

This book would not be possible without my partnership with KitchenAid. Thank you for allowing us to showcase your wonderful products.

Thank you to Jennifer Smith, Michelle Meade, and the entire Figure 1 team for the collaborative partnership. I am grateful for your outstanding support throughout the process.

Bennett, Brodie, and Tate, I hope that one day you get to cook with these recipes to create your own special stories and experiences through food—all of which can be shared with your own family and loved ones. Thank you for being such an inspiration.

A career in the kitchen can be very demanding and too often we rely on our loved ones to help us make it through. Above all, I am indebted to Charlene, my amazing wife and best friend, who has been there for me at the best and worst of times. As an incredible mother and wife, you go above and beyond duty to support our beautiful family. Thank you for your unwavering support through this long journey—I do all of this because of you.

INDEX

CONVERSION CHARTS

Volume

Imperial	Metric
⅛ tsp	0.5 ml
¼ tsp	1 ml
½ tsp	2.5 ml
¾ tsp	4 ml
1 tsp	5 ml
½ Tbsp	8 ml
1 Tbsp	15 ml
1½ Tbsp	23 ml
2 Tbsp	30 ml
¼ cup	60 ml
⅓ cup	80 ml
½ cup	125 ml
⅔ cup	165 ml
¾ cup	185 ml
1 cup	250 ml
1¼ cups	310 ml
1⅓ cups	330 ml
1½ cups	375 ml
1⅔ cups	415 ml
1¾ cups	435 ml
2 cups	500 ml
2¼ cups	560 ml
2⅓ cups	580 ml
2½ cups	625 ml
2¾ cups	690 ml
3 cups	750 ml
4 cups/1 qt	1 L
5 cups	1.25 L
6 cups	1.5 L
7 cups	1.75 L
8 cups	2 L

Weight

Imperial	Metric
½ oz	15 g
1 oz	30 g
2 oz	60 g
3 oz	85 g
4 oz (¼ lb)	115 g
5 oz	140 g
6 oz	170 g
7 oz	200 g
8 oz (½ lb)	225 g
9 oz	255 g
10 oz	285 g
11 oz	310 g
12 oz (¾ lb)	340 g
13 oz	370 g
14 oz	400 g
15 oz	425 g
16 oz (1 lb)	450 g
1¼ lb	570 g
1½ lb	670 g
2 lb	900 g
3 lb	1.4 kg
4 lb	1.8 kg
5 lb	2.3 kg
6 lb	2.7 kg

Liquid measures

Imperial	Metric
1 fl oz	30 ml
2 fl oz	60 ml
3 fl oz	90 ml
4 fl oz	120 ml

Linear

Imperial	Metric
⅛ inch	3 mm
¼ inch	6 mm
½ inch	12 mm
¾ inch	2 cm
1 inch	2.5 cm
1¼ inches	3 cm
1½ inches	3.5 cm
1¾ inches	4.5 cm
2 inches	5 cm
2½ inches	6.5 cm
3 inches	7.5 cm
4 inches	10 cm
5 inches	12.5 cm
6 inches	15 cm
8 inches	20 cm
10 inches	25 cm
12 inches	30 cm
13 inches	33 cm
16 inches	41 cm
18 inches	46 cm

Baking pans

Imperial	Metric
5 × 9-inch loaf pan	2 L loaf pan
9 × 13-inch cake pan	4 L cake pan
11 × 17-inch baking sheet	30 × 45-cm baking sheet

Cans & jars

Imperial	Metric
6 oz	170 g
28 oz	796 ml

Oven temperature

Imperial	Metric
200°F	95°C
250°F	120°C
275°F	135°C
300°F	150°C
325°F	160°C
350°F	180°C
375°F	190°C
400°F	200°C
425°F	220°C
450°F	230°C

Temperature

Imperial	Metric
90°F	32°C
120°F	49°C
125°F	52°C
130°F	54°C
140°F	60°C
150°F	66°C
155°F	68°C
160°F	71°C
165°F	74°C
170°F	77°C
175°F	80°C
180°F	82°C
190°F	88°C
200°F	93°C
240°F	116°C
250°F	121°C
300°F	149°C
325°F	163°C
350°F	177°C
360°F	182°C
375°F	191°C

ABOUT US

Corbin's passion for food and family runs deep. Raised on a farm outside of Edmonton, Alberta, one of his earliest memories is the smell of baking bread in his grandmother's kitchen. With 30 years of culinary experience, Corbin has worked at some of the world's largest hotels and was the host of Food Network shows such as *Dinner Party Wars*, *Restaurant Takeover*, and *The Incredible Food Race*. He is also an active member of the Canadian Federation of Chefs and Cooks, is an ambassador for KitchenAid, and volunteers for organizations including the Canadian Cancer Society, the Heart and Stroke Foundation of Canada, and Osteoporosis Canada. His first cookbook, *In Good Company*, celebrates his philosophy of food, fun, and family. He currently lives in Toronto with his wife and three sons.

Instagram **@chefcorbin1**
Twitter **@chefcorbin**
Facebook **Chef Corbin**

Karen Geier is a Toronto-based writer and food enthusiast. When she's not working on fermentation and bread experiments in her urban kitchen, Karen writes for media outlets like *The Guardian* and corporate clients. With Corbin, Karen has written over 100 articles on cooking.